PARENTCARE SURVIVAL GUIDE

Helping Your Folks Through the

Not-So-Golden Years

by
Enid Pritikin, M.S.W., L.C.S.W.
and
Trudy Reece, M.S.O.T.

BARRON'S

All inquiries should be addressed to:
Barron's Educational Series, Inc.
250 Wireless Boulevard
Hauppauge, New York 11788

Library of Congress Catalog Card No. 92-35544
International Standard Book No. 0-8120-4975-6

Library of Congress Cataloging-in-Publication Data

Pritikin, Enid.
    Parentcare survival guide: coping with the not-so-golden years/
by Enid Pritikin and Trudy Reece.
        p.   cm.
    Includes bibliographical references and index.
    ISBN 0-8120-4975-6
    1. Parent and adult child—United States.   2. Aging Parents—
United States—Family relationships.   3. Aged—Care—
United States.
    I. Reece, Trudy.   II. Title.
    HQ775.86.P75   1993
    306.874—dc20

                                                          92-35544
                                                               CIP

PRINTED IN THE UNITED STATES OF AMERICA
3456   5100   987654321

To our parents

David and Zelda Fields
and
Macky and Betty Sanders

So far, we've needed you
a whole lot more than you've needed us.

Acknowledgments

This book owes its existence to many wonderful people, and to them we're deeply grateful. First off, we'd like to thank all of the hundreds of families who shared their lives and experiences with Enid and, in doing so, contributed immeasurably to this book.

We also thank Angela M. Thoburn, M.A., for giving Enid the shove she needed; Josh Pritikin for providing ace computer consultation; Jenina Deshler, M.S.W., Madelyn Silver Palley, M.Sc., Ilene Pritikin, Jane Reece, Ph.D., Rosemary Sanders, M.F.A., Alex J. Weinstein, M.D., Helen Wong, R.N., and Katina Zaninovich, R.N. for generously providing assistance in the early stages; and Rene Brochester, Stephanie Feingold, Zelda Fields, Helena Kennedy, Ellen McGinty King, Ethan Reece, Macky Sanders, Richard Sanders, and Bob Silverman for their valuable feedback at various points along the way.

For their indispensible expertise, we thank Ella Aaberg, Kathy Badrak, Hazel Brewer, R.N., Robert Cibull, D.O., Jeffrey Comins, Ph.D., Louise A. Currey, R.N., David S. Fields, Ph.D., John S. Gardner, M.A., Lois Hanson, Patricia Hanson, R.P.T., Alan R. Hersh, M.D., Gary Imlay, M.S.W., Mary Lou La Barge, R.N., joyce ellen lippman, M.P.A., Mary McNally, R.N., Charles H. Nicholson, M.D.,

Catherine Lee Ross, Stephen Stone, M.S.W., Susan Stone, Esq., and Marilyn Yeates, M.S.W. And we especially thank Grace Hampton, M.S.W. for valiantly reading the entire manuscript and Daniel J. Fields, M.D. for the endless telephone consultations at all hours of the day and night.

We'd also like to express our appreciation to our agent Julian Bach for continuing to believe in us and in this project and to our editors at Barron's—Grace Freedson, Judy Makover, Carolyn Horne, and Max Reed—for their most helpful guidance and forbearance.

To our husbands, David Stoms and Jeff Reece, who rescued us from computer hell, served as constant sounding boards, and were (mostly) supportive in the face of terrible neglect, we owe much more than mere thanks. And last but not least, two special commendations go to Noah Pritikin and Naomi Reece for tolerating two distracted, mean mommies for an awfully long time.

E.P. and T.R.

When a father helps a son, both smile;
When a son must help his father, both cry.

Yiddish Folk Saying

Table of Contents

▼

Why This Book?

You're probably aware of the statistics. The number of people over age sixty-five is growing like crazy, and more people than ever before are living to be very old. In fact, for the first time in the history of this country, the average couple has more parents than children.

Not only are people living longer, but those who were once considered to be getting on in years themselves are now finding that they must care for an even older generation. Every day, more and more elderly people are becoming dependent on their adult children.

That means you.

But helping aging parents has become more complicated than it used to be because our society has undergone some big changes during the past few decades.

- Parents don't live with their children in extended families the way they used to.

- Many people are starting families later in life and are ending up with both parents *and* children who need their attention at the same time, thus the term "sandwich generation."

- Women are entering the work force in record numbers and aren't available to be caregivers the way they have been.

- Because the birthrate has decreased, many elderly people have fewer offspring to help care for them.

- Families are living farther apart now than in past generations.

- The divorce rate has risen, which has put an additional strain on people's time, money, and energy.

Despite these complications, you and millions of other adult children are bending over backwards, throwing your lives into chaos, and making considerable sacrifices as you struggle to be there for your folks. At times, the problems seem insurmountable.

What if your mother refuses to move from her home when there's no doubt that it's unsafe for her to stay there? What if your only sibling is so involved in his career that he won't pitch in and help your parents, even though he lives just as close to them as you do? What if your widowed father has sold his house and furniture and has moved in with you; then a few months later, you realize that you've made a terrible mistake?

The *Parentcare Survival Guide* offers a sensible, realistic approach to dealing with these kinds of difficult dilemmas. Although this book specifically addresses children of aging parents, it can also help those who have aunts, uncles, grandparents, spouses, and elderly friends who need assistance. We wrote it because we know that you can do your best for your folks without becoming overwhelmed, and that with the right approach, the challenge of parentcare can be met.

Part I

The Basics

Chapter

1

Meeting up with the Parentcare Predicament

Mothering was what Betty had always done best. She was a housewife who had spent her entire adult life taking care of her husband and their four children. When the last child left home, Betty felt useless and lonely in the empty house all day. So she made up her mind to do something that she'd thought about doing for years—she enrolled in her local state college as a part-time student. She was surprised to discover that not only could she do the work, but she was having the time of her life.

One day she was sitting at her kitchen table finishing a term paper when she got an alarming phone call. It was the owner of the doughnut shop where her father Ollie had coffee with his buddies every morning. He told her that her father had collapsed a few minutes earlier and had been rushed by ambulance to the hospital.

Betty was out the door in a flash.

When your folks get older they'll inevitably begin to experience some problems, and this may be the first time in many years that you become closely involved in their lives.

When you were a baby, you were intimately tied to your parents. You were dependent on them for survival, and they were all you needed or wanted. As you moved through childhood you began the slow process of separation, and as you entered adolescence you started to work seriously on declaring your independence from them. Then you finally made it to young adulthood when you were out in the world on your own.

For a number of years now, you've probably been pretty busy living your own life. On holidays or birthdays you're very likely to call your parents or visit them. And if they live nearby, you undoubtedly see them more often. Whatever the specifics of the arrangement, your relationship with them has settled into a fairly comfortable routine.

But then, you get the Dreaded Phone Call...and everything changes.

When Betty got to the emergency room, she was told by a nurse that her father had suffered a stroke and that the doctors were still trying to determine how severe it was. Betty called her husband who said that he'd be right over, and she left a phone message with her brother who lived in a neighboring state.

There was nothing else she could do except sit in the waiting room. Her mother had died of cancer 15 years earlier in this hospital, and Betty was flooded with bad memories of the place. She had a close, warm relationship with her father, and she didn't want to lose him.

Finally, the doctor came out. He told her that the stroke had been a moderate one, that Ollie was stable, and that he'd probably pull through. It would be several months before they'd know the full extent of any permanent damage.

As soon as she saw her dad, Betty could tell that he was in pretty bad shape. He couldn't speak clearly, the right side of his face drooped, and he seemed terrified. All she could do was squeeze his hand and promise that she'd take good care of him. She was thankful that he was going to make it, but she also felt apprehensive. She knew that he'd need her now as he never had before, and she wondered how all of this was going to affect her life.

The Losses of Aging

Everybody faces changes with age—the wrinkles, the graying and thinning hair, the difficulty in reading small print, the decrease in endurance, and all of the other undeniable reminders of the passage of time. However, as people get into their later years, the losses of aging become much more significant. For one thing, there are many more of them. And for another thing, they can seriously affect people's ability to manage their lives independently. Of course, every person's experience is different, and many elderly people lead active, satisfying, and thoroughly fulfilling lives. But loss is still the one thing that all older people have in common.

- Their strength and stamina probably aren't what they used to be, and so they may have difficulty getting around as easily as they did in the past. In addition, they may have trouble performing some of the basic activities of daily living, such as bathing, dressing, cooking, and cleaning.

- It's likely that their eyesight, hearing, and sense of taste and smell all have begun to fade. These changes no doubt are annoying to them. But these things also may have affected their ability to communicate with other people and to go about their lives safely.

- They may experience disturbing changes in their usual sleep patterns. It may take them longer to fall asleep than it did in the past. They may not sleep as soundly as they used to. They may wake up more often during the night. And they may awaken very early in the morning.

- They may be going through the humiliation and inconvenience of poor bladder control.

- They may be troubled with chronic constipation.

- The slowing of their sexual response (and perhaps the absence of a partner) may be an unwelcome change.

- They may have gone through a sudden, frightening health crisis, such as a heart attack, a stroke, a broken hip, or a diagnosis of cancer.

- They may suffer from chronic, debilitating health problems that have gotten worse over the years. This could include arthritis, heart disease, emphysema, adult-onset diabetes, prostate problems, cataracts, Parkinson's disease, dental problems, foot problems, or any number of other conditions.

- They may be troubled by annoying memory problems. Or they may even suffer from dementia.

- They may be having particular difficulty adjusting to their losses, and so they may be doubly burdened with debilitating emotional problems and possibly with the problem of substance abuse as well.

- They may have had to stop driving, and sorely miss the independence that it gave them.

- They may have been victims of a crime such as a theft, which has left them traumatized and fearful.

- If they've retired from longtime jobs, they've most likely lost a vital source of their personal identity, self-esteem, and sense of purpose.

- Because of inflation and the ups and downs of the business world, the retirement planning that was supposed to get them through their later years may not have worked out as they hoped it would. As a consequence, their financial security may be shaky, and they may have trouble getting by on a fixed income. This can be especially hard if they have large medical bills as well as the extra expense of hiring the help that may be needed.

- They may have been through the devastating loss of a spouse. This may have left them feeling especially adrift if they were married for many years and if the two of them functioned as a team.

- Their social support system may be crumbling as other family members and friends die or move away.

- They may have had to deal with the death of a beloved pet, a loss that could have been harder on them than anyone thought it would be.

- If they've been in the same home for many years, they may have gradually discovered that the neighborhood has changed and their community no longer feels familiar to them anymore.

- If they've moved out of their home, they've lost not only the house itself and possibly some of their treasured possessions, but also their neighbors and the familiar routines and responsibilities that gave order and meaning to their lives.

There's no question about it. The losses of aging are formidable indeed, and the so-called Golden Years can turn out to be Not-So-Golden, after all.

Ollie stayed in the hospital for a week, and from there he went to a rehabilitation center where he received physical, occupational, and speech therapy for three more weeks. Eventually, he was able to walk with a walker and do all of his own self-care with the use of his good hand. His speech improved too, but sometimes he had trouble expressing himself as well as he wanted, and he got discouraged and frustrated easily.

He was much more relaxed when Betty was around. She understood everything he said, and she anticipated his needs better than anyone else did. Because her dad brightened up when-

ever she walked in the room, Betty spent as much time with him as she could.

Betty's husband wasn't thrilled that he hardly ever saw her, but she kept assuring him that the situation was only temporary. For now, she knew that she had to be with her father.

When your folks turn to you for help, your first impulse probably will be to drop everything and do what you can for them.

But it won't always be easy.

You have other important demands on your time. In addition to your work and your other responsibilities, you may have children at home to care for. Or your kids may be leaving the nest and you must deal with the impact of this major change on your life. Then again, your offspring may be coming *back* home just when you thought they were finally ready to make it on their own. Or you may have your own worrisome health problems. And on top of this, your spouse may resent all you're doing for your parents.

Yet, despite all of the challenges that you're facing, your middle years hold out a great deal of promise. This could be the time when you're finally in a position to kick back and to start realizing some of your own dreams that have been on the back burner for years. You may have more financial security than you've had in the past, so some new options may have opened up for you. You could decide to pursue a new career, take a long-planned vacation, or get involved in an exciting new hobby. You may be considering a major move in preparation for retirement. Or you may be eagerly looking forward to enjoying your grandchildren. There's a whole world of possibilities out there.

Being unexpectedly tied down to your parents and their problems doesn't fit particularly well into your plans. The timing is often terrible, and this intrusion into your life usually stems from some unpleasant realities that you'd rather not think about. You want your folks to be strong and capable, and it's probably painful for you to discover that they need your help. You knew that this kind of thing happened to other people's aging parents, but you may have hoped that it wouldn't happen to your folks—at least, not yet.

When Ollie came home, his apartment was set up with all kinds of special equipment so that he could do everything he needed to do safely and independently. Therapists from a home health agency came in a few times a week to continue working with him, and he was equipped with a personal emergency response system, so if he got into trouble he could get help immediately.

Betty stayed with him quite a bit during the first few days to help him with the transition. She'd leave him alone for short periods of time to go home, run errands, or attend a class, and he'd be fine. But when she got ready to leave him for his first night alone, he got an anxious look on his face. And when he started to speak, his speech sounded just like it did right after his stroke.

Betty asked him if he was all right, and he admitted that he did feel a little scared. She didn't want to leave him when he was obviously so worried, so she decided to stay another night. But one night turned into two, and two nights turned into three. She kept hoping each night that he'd be ready to stay alone. But he never was.

Two weeks later, she was still spending her nights at her father's place.

Her husband was getting annoyed and was convinced that she was spoiling Ollie. Her brother, who called every day, offered to pay for someone to come in and help Betty out. She considered this but decided that it was silly to hire someone just to sleep over. She wasn't happy with the situation either, and she was starting to resent her father. She also felt guilty that she was neglecting her husband and her schoolwork. But she didn't want to upset her dad or let him down.

She wanted everyone to be happy. But how could she make it happen?

You love your folks, you want to help them out, and you want everyone to think that you're a nice person. But you may also feel resentful that your parents are having problems, that they expect so much from you, and that you feel such a strong sense of responsibility toward them.

Sooner or later it may become clear to you that no matter how hard you try, you're not going to be able to find answers that satisfy everyone. As you think about the options that are available to your folks, you may discover that many of them have serious drawbacks or are downright terrible. Moreover, one person in the family might think that a certain plan is reasonable and worth looking into, while someone else may think that it would never work. You want to come up with a wonderful solution that will please everyone. But you can't.

This is the Parentcare Predicament.

A few days later, Betty walked one of the therapists to his car. She told him she wished there was some way she could get her father to feel comfortable staying alone at night.

He was surprised to hear that she'd been staying with Ollie all night and told her that there was no reason why he couldn't stay by himself.

Betty confessed that it was partly her own fault. She didn't have the heart to leave him alone because she knew how frightened he was.

The therapist suggested that Betty might want to speak to the agency social worker who dealt with problems like this all the time. Betty thought that sounded like a good idea. At this point, she was willing to try almost anything.

A Few Facts of Life

In order to come to grips with the parentcare predicament, you'll have to learn to accept a few painful facts of life.

First, there's the fact that loss is unavoidable. The losses of aging are inescapable and inevitable. You may be able to help your folks reduce the impact of certain kinds of problems, but there's no way you can eliminate the problems altogether. Unfortunately, bad stuff happens to everybody, and nobody can take good fortune for granted. Sooner or later, everyone will experience setbacks and even painful tragedies.

Furthermore, there's the fact that change is one of life's few constants. Uncertainty is one of the few things that everyone can always count on. Nothing is permanent, and no one can assume that things will continue on as they always have.

And finally, there's the fact that no one can do it all. There's just so much time in the day, and there's a limit to how much physical and emotional energy any one person can expend. No one can be everything to everybody.

The Bottom Line

There are rarely any easy answers. Most of the time, the best you can do is settle on the Least-Lousy Solution that meets everyone's needs—somewhat.

When your folks need your help for a short period of time, you probably can drop everything and do what's necessary for them, and there won't be any real conflict for you. But if your parents continue to require your help, you may soon find that you're running into trouble. You can manage to make certain sacrifices, you can ignore your other responsibilities, and you can put aside the needs of the other people in your life—but only for a limited time. You won't be able to keep it up for long. Very soon, those other demands will start vying for your attention.

The only way to deal with this dilemma is to acknowledge that you can't please everyone. If you try, you'll only end up doing less than your best for all the people in your life—including yourself.

A few days later, Betty, her husband, and her father met with the social worker in Ollie's living room. The social worker told them that these kinds of adjustments were often very difficult for families.

She asked Ollie how things were going for him. He looked at her a little warily and said that they were going all right.

Then she asked Betty's husband for his input. He said that he thought that Betty was trying to do too much and that he wanted to see her back home again.

Then it was Betty's turn. She hesitantly explained that it wasn't working well for her to be at her father's so much. She wanted to spend more time at home, but she felt uneasy leaving Ollie alone at night.

Ollie said that he knew that it wasn't fair for Betty to be spending so much time with him.

The social worker asked him what he was afraid might happen if he spent the night alone. He thought for awhile and admitted that he couldn't think of anything. Then she asked him gently if he thought that it might be time to give it a try. After all, he was going to have to start doing it eventually. He looked around for a few moments and agreed that it made sense to try.

Betty looked at her father nervously and assured him that she'd still help him with his bills and with his shopping and that she'd still stop by every day and bring him his evening meal.

She hoped that she wasn't being too hard on her dad.

Settling on Least-Lousy Solutions can be nerve-racking and unsatisfying, and sometimes it can be downright depressing. It may upset you to know that things probably will not get resolved happily and cleanly, no matter how much effort you put into it. You may wish the answer would come easily. But chances are that it won't.

In order to settle on the solution, everyone will have to make some sacrifices as well as some serious compromises. Every person who's involved in the situation will have to give a little, and sometimes a lot. It may not be fair that you're being forced to choose to meet the needs of one person over the needs of another. But that's the way it is when there are no easy answers.

That night, Ollie spent the night by himself. Betty phoned to check on him more often than she should have, and she was so tense that her husband wondered if they should have just left things the way they were.

But as time went on, she and her father eventually got used to the arrangement, and Betty was able to get on with her life.

Betty was lucky in many ways. She had a good relationship with her father, and he was basically a reasonable man. She had a supportive husband who understood her need to be with her dad and who was willing to tolerate it up to a point. She no longer had kids at home to contend with. Her brother was concerned and tried to do what he could from afar. And the family had expert advice in setting up Ollie's apartment and in training him so that he could remain at home safely.

But not every problem is quite as straightforward as Betty's. As you move through this book, you'll learn how to find your own Least-Lousy Solution.

Chapter 2

Looking Out for Yourself

Malcolm was an only child who had one exasperating problem that was always lurking in the corner of his mind. It was his mother, Samantha.

Samantha was an utterly self-absorbed woman who'd been spoiled and pampered all of her life—first by her parents, then by her three older brothers, and finally by her husband. Deep down inside she felt dissatisfied with herself, and consequently she was very critical of others—especially of her son. For as long as Malcolm could remember, his mother never lost an opportunity to let him know what a disappointment he was.

Because Malcolm could never please his difficult mother, he invariably felt tense and on guard when he was with her. But because he was brought up to respect his elders, he did his best to get along. And as long as his father was around, he managed to maintain a cordial—though somewhat distant—relationship with her. By keeping his visits as short as possible, he gave her as few opportunities as he could to make the cutting remarks that hurt him so much.

Then Malcolm's father died suddenly of a heart attack.

As soon as Malcolm heard the news, he got a sinking feeling

14

in the pit of his stomach. His mother was going to be alone for the first time in her life. She had many acquaintances, but no real friends, and she'd depended on his father for virtually everything. He knew that she was going to expect much more from him now than she had in the past.

Since there are so many different kinds of problems that can come up as people age, there's no way that you can ever fully prepare yourself for the time when your folks will need you. So, if you're like most adult children, you've probably given little thought to what your responsibilities will be toward them. What usually happens is that you fall right into step and do what you think you should do—or what you think others think you should do.

It may be that your efforts serve everyone just fine. Your parents may get the attention that they require, and you may feel good that you're able to help them. But it may also happen that your spontaneous caregiving style doesn't work out so well. Old family dynamics and behavior patterns from childhood could come back to haunt you, and you might find yourself getting into one or more of the Potentially Troublesome Routines that caregivers are prone to.

In moderation, these routines can serve everyone nicely. But if you don't watch out, they can easily get out of hand.

Some Potentially Troublesome Routines

You Like to Be in Control

Some people like to be in charge at all times. They think that they're the only ones who can do the job right. So they unwittingly scare off their siblings and any other people who are willing to help by criticizing them and undermining their efforts. They insist on running the show, often ending up with all the responsibility themselves. And they usually resent it.

You're Afraid to Stand Up for Yourself

Some people are afraid of saying no to their parents because they're terrified that their folks might get angry with them. So they pander to their parents, they ignore their own needs, and they throw their own lives into chaos. Then they end up taking out their frustration on others around them.

You Tend to Be a Mother Hen

Some people find it very satisfying to smother their parents with excessive care because they themselves so badly need to be needed. They do their best to see to it that their folks become dependent on them. Then, in order to finally get themselves out from under all the responsibility, they have to find an unassailable excuse, such as becoming physically ill.

You're a Little Too Close to Your Parents

Some people have never really separated from their folks. They're extremely close to them, and their relationship with them is one of mutual dependence. They don't think they're capable of standing on their own two feet, and so they never get around to cutting the apron strings. As a result, they may forgo the opportunity to forge their own separate identities. And because of this, they never become independent adults.

You're Convinced That You Can Do Just About Anything You Set Your Mind To

Some people think that they can do it all. So they proceed to try to do just that. Consequently, they often end up doing less than their best for everyone—especially themselves.

You Want to Make Amends for the Past

Some people see themselves as less-than-perfect and have a special need to redeem themselves in the eyes of their parents. So they try with all their might to prove their worth to their folks. But no matter what they do, their parents may still never quite believe in them the way they'd like them to.

You Feel Beholden to Your Parents

Some people are either accepting money from their parents or else they've been informed that there will be a windfall waiting for them down the line. Therefore, their relationship with their folks has strings attached. They may knock themselves out doing exactly what their benefactors want them to, but their relationship with their parents never becomes one of equals.

You're Stuck in the Old Guilt Routine

Guilt is the one issue that people most often bring up when they seek help in dealing with aging parents. Those who suffer from it think they are fundamentally inadequate because they aren't making their parents happy, and they're furious at themselves because they continue to try—even though they know it's hopeless.

There are two kinds of guilt. Healthy, normal guilt is what people feel when they've done something that they shouldn't have done. They know it wasn't right and they regret doing it. If they apologize, try to make amends, and learn something from the experience, their sense of remorse will eventually go away—or at least it will become less all-consuming. This kind of guilt serves a worthwhile purpose.

The Old Guilt Routine is something else altogether. It's closely connected to the sense of inadequacy and low self-esteem that burden many people. Those who are locked into it feel guilty no matter what they do.

They get into this routine when they're small children, when the one thing they want more than anything else in the world is to please their parents. But their parents don't communicate with them in a straightforward and honest fashion. Instead, they manipulate them by playing the role of the perennially injured party. When these children do something that displeases their folks, the parents take the behavior as a personal affront, act as though they're being treated badly, and insist that they deserve better. Their message is that if their kids really loved them, they'd behave in a certain way.

But there will always be times when children don't live up to their folks' expectations. And when parents continually act as though their offspring have let them down, their children's precarious sense of self-esteem can become eroded. Eventually, these children find that there's no real connection between how much they're doing for their parents and the amount of guilt they're feeling. They feel guilty about all the things they could be doing, whether these things are actually expected of them or not. Often they become even harder on themselves than their parents are. Then, when their folks get older and become physically or mentally infirm, they find new opportunities to berate themselves for not doing enough. And even after their parents are dead, they may agonize to themselves that if only they'd done this or that, things would have been different.

Underneath the Old Guilt Routine are other emotions. There's anger, there's hurt, and there's sadness. And hidden under all of that is love, or at least a longing for it, but it's not easy to experience love when it's buried under so many uncomfortable feelings.

Just as Malcolm had feared, his mother turned to him constantly after his father's death. She was lonely. Could he stop by for a bit? She needed to get out. Would he take her to a nice place to eat? She was ignorant about business matters. Could he keep an eye on her financial affairs?

Malcolm did his best to help her because he knew that he was all she had. But it didn't take long before the strain of being around her began to get to him. He felt like a fool the way he fawned all over her, and it infuriated him the way she always managed to find some little fault with virtually everything he did. He resented the overwhelming sense of obligation he felt toward her, but he had no idea how to free himself from it.

His frustration was slowly building. He never smiled or laughed anymore, and he constantly found himself ruminating over conversations he'd either had or would like to have with his mother. At home he was withdrawn and silent; and at work he was distracted and irritable. He was losing weight because he had no appetite. He had difficulty sleeping. He began to look forward to more than a few beers before dinner (and especially before going to see his mother). And he had a stomachache much of the time.

It can be very hard to say no to your folks. After all, they're the ones who cared for you all those years. You probably feel that—at the very least—you owe them something. But as you help them out, you may find that you're doing things grudgingly for them—that there's a discrepancy between what you really want to do and what you're actually doing. When this is the case, you can easily end up feeling resentful, bitter, and put upon.

When you're experiencing these kinds of negative feelings, it means that things have gotten out of hand. Everyone can live with some aggravation and stress, but there are limits to how much people can tolerate. The important thing to realize is that your feelings never lie. They tell the truth whether you like it or not, and they won't go away just because you want them to or because you try to ignore them. When you keep your negative feelings locked up inside and when you refuse to listen to what they're trying to tell you, they fester away and siphon off precious energy. Eventually they come out in insidious and destructive ways.

Some Signs That Things Have Gotten out of Hand

You Spend Your Time Obsessing

Your pent up emotions haunt you so powerfully that you lie awake at night worrying, and you go around in circles with your obsessive thoughts. You feel overwhelmed, frustrated, angry, lonely, panicky, nervous, frightened, depressed, out of control, or at the end of your rope. You may wish that your parent would die so that all of your problems would be solved. You may desperately want to withdraw or escape. You may even think about suicide.

You Have Trouble Concentrating

Because you're obsessing much of the time, you're preoccupied, distracted, and accident-prone. You tune out when others are talking because you're so involved with your own thoughts. You miss your exit as you drive along the freeway. You cut yourself with a knife when you're preparing dinner.

You Try to Blot Out Your Feelings

You deal with your uncomfortable feelings by attempting to deny them altogether. You try to numb or distract yourself by indulging in addictive or self-destructive behaviors, such as overeating, overwork, compulsive sex, or alcohol or drug abuse.

Your Body Is Falling Apart

Your body is sending out signals like crazy in an effort to try to force you to pay attention to your feelings. You grind your teeth. You have headaches. There's tension in your neck or back. Or you're tired all the time. When complaints like these occur, you should check with a doctor to make sure that there's no underlying disease. But very often these symptoms are your body's response to the aggravation that you're feeling.

Your Relationships Are Out of Kilter

Your suppressed feelings are playing havoc with your relationships. The first ones who are affected are the people you live with, the ones you care about the most. You lose your sense of humor along with your temper. You're irritable and hypercritical. You're unwilling to listen to anyone else's point of view. And as things get further out of control, your anger and frustration spill over into your relationships outside of your immediate family. Eventually, you may alienate others in your life and find yourself becoming increasingly isolated.

You Become a Whiner

You complain to anyone who'll listen to you. You work hard to impress others with gruesome tales of the sacrifices you're making and the aggravation you're enduring. At first you may get a lot of attention when you gripe like this. But sooner or later you may notice that almost everyone you know is sick and tired of being around you.

You Take Justice into Your Own Hands

Because you feel put upon, you look for your own ways of imposing justice. Instead of telling your siblings that you need them to help you out more, you sneak around and quietly take valuables from your parents' home to pay yourself back for all your work. Or you persuade your folks to sign a legal document without their full understanding of its implications. Obviously, this kind of surreptitious behavior is unethical if not illegal.

21

You Take It Out on Your Folks

You're oversolicitous and phony with your parents because you're trying to hide your anger. Or you're sarcastic with them as you attempt to cover up your resentment. You subconsciously want to punish them, so you constantly forget to do the things you promised to do. Or you ignore their needs entirely and stay away from them because you can't bear to confront the difficult feelings that they elicit in you.

You may even get to the point where you're totally out of control and your behavior borders on elder-abuse. You angrily respond to your mom's fourth request to be helped to the bathroom at night by yanking her up with a tighter-than-necessary grip and shoving her down the hall to hurry her along. You threaten her that if she doesn't eat, you'll have her force-fed. You go on a day trip knowing full well that she can't move and that she'll have to lie in the same position for hours with no way to summon help. And your behavior may become so abusive that you cause physical harm.

The age-old, shameful problem of elder-abuse cuts across social, racial, religious, and economic lines. Ironically, many victims of elder-abuse live with their abusing children. Abused parents often suffer in silence because they're too ashamed to tell anyone what's happening, because they're afraid of being abandoned, or because they believe they deserve poor treatment. When children continually abuse their folks, there's usually a history of poor relationships in the family, and they may be repaying their parents for ill treatment suffered while they were growing up. And not infrequently, substance abuse or mental illness is involved.

Six months had passed since his father's death. Malcolm's stomach pains were becoming more frequent and severe, and his stools were definitely not normal. He tried to ignore these unpleas-

ant developments for as long as he could, but one morning he woke up with such a terrible burning pain in his stomach that he could hardly get himself out of bed. When he managed to stand up, he felt lightheaded and nearly fainted.

On the insistence of his wife, Malcolm went to see his physician that afternoon. The doctor immediately suspected that he had a bleeding ulcer. The next day, the results of a few tests came back, and the diagnosis was officially confirmed. The physician prescribed an ulcer regimen and also gave him a list of therapists with a strong recommendation that he get psychological counseling. He warned Malcolm that if he didn't get his ulcer under control, it could be fatal.

In your urgency to make things better for your folks, you can lose track of your own feelings. One day you may look in the mirror and see dark circles under your eyes. You're feeling overwhelmed and frazzled. The signs are everywhere. What are you supposed to do?

The Bottom Line

You absolutely must look after yourself. That's the only way you can do your best for your folks, for your other loved ones...and for yourself.

How to Feel Less Frazzled

When your day-to-day routines are no longer working, the time has come for you to find new ways to interact with your parents. You're the one who will have to take steps to do things differently. You can't expect them to make any changes themselves. Chances are, they're quite content with the arrangement as it is. But there are some things you can do to improve your situation.

Identify Your Potentially Troublesome Routines

Step back, look at yourself, and examine your behavior with an objective eye. Ask yourself why you're doing what you are doing. Try to figure out what the payoff is for you. What are you looking for? Love? Attention? Approval? Pity? Praise? Money?

These questions may not be easy to ask, and the answers may be difficult to figure out. But if you're willing to own up to what's really going on, you finally can begin to stop doing the things that give you so much aggravation. Then if you choose to, you can find healthier ways of interacting with your parents.

Pay Attention to Your Feelings and Acknowledge Your Limits

Keep in mind that your emotions are indicators that can help you correct your behavior. They're telling you that your routines have gone too far and that it's time to slow down, to get out, or to try something else altogether. Remember that you're entitled to feel the way you do. Don't punish yourself because of your feelings. They're your authentic, spontaneous reactions to the situation.

Once you know what you can and cannot tolerate, you need to decide what it is that's reasonable and comfortable for you to be doing for your parents at this time in your life.

Stand Up for Yourself

You may want to talk with your parents about the changes that you're making. Or, you may prefer to simply start behaving differently. What you must do is set a new plan for yourself, and consistently, clearly, and thoughtfully follow through on it. Keep in mind that lifelong habits are tough to change and that this won't happen overnight. It will be a gradual process, there will be setbacks, and sometimes your old routines will tempt you. Your parents may not be happy with the arrangement at first, but eventually they'll adjust.

Learn to Say No to Your Parents

When you need to say no to your parents, the message inside your words should be that you love them even though you may not be doing exactly what they want you to do. You can give a simple, straightforward explanation for your decision. Or you can suggest another way of honoring the request. But you don't need to make excuses for yourself. This is because you're doing what's right for you. When you say no, maintain eye contact, and say it firmly and calmly. Instead of saying:

Well…okay, Mom. I have a lot going on. But I guess I can come by and take you shopping.

You can say:

No, Mom. I can't come by today. But I'd be glad to take you shopping on Saturday when I've got more time.

Don't Attempt to Be a Mind Reader

You shouldn't assume that your folks instinctively know what you're thinking and feeling. If you want them to know, you've got to tell them. Similarly, you shouldn't presume to know what they're thinking or feeling. You've got to ask them. Don't fall into the trap of doing what you think they expect of you when that may not be what they want at all. Instead of saying:

All right, Mother. I guess I'd better fix dinner for you if you're so tired.

You can say:

Mother, I'm not sure if you're asking me to fix dinner for you, or if you just want me to know what a hard day you've had.

Be Direct

Instead of hiding your real agenda behind a question or an ambivalent statement, tell your folks clearly and directly what it is that you want. Instead of saying:

Your friends do their own marketing, don't they?

You can say:

Mom, it would really make things easier on me if you'd ask one of your friends to take you to the market with her when she goes.

Try to Avoid Using the Words Always and Never

When you use these words, you're usually exaggerating. And besides, they often set an accusatory tone and put your parents on the defensive. Instead of saying:

I don't believe it, Ma. You're always throwing out important papers.

You can say:

> *Ma, if you want me to help you with your bills, please put your mail in a box so I can find all of them.*

Instead of Making Accusations, Share Your Feelings

It only makes common sense that your parents will be more responsive to suggestions, complaints, or criticisms if these kinds of remarks are made in a nonthreatening, upbeat manner. So, try to identify the specific behavior that's bothering you, tell your parents how the behavior makes you feel, and then discuss what could be done differently the next time. This way the criticism becomes constructive. Instead of saying:

> *Really, Mom. I have my own life, you know. So, please stop calling me at the last minute.*

You can say:

> *Mom, I really feel hassled when you ask me to do things at the last minute. I'd be happy to take you to the doctor, but please check with me before you make the appointment.*

Give Specific, Positive Feedback

When your parents are doing something that is helpful, tell them how much you appreciate it. This will encourage more of the same. Instead of saying nothing, you can say:

> *Gee, Mom, it means so much to me when you make the effort to be ready when I pick you up.*

If Necessary, Limit Your Contact with Your Folks

If your parents manage to push all your buttons whenever you're around them, perhaps you should limit the amount of time you spend with them. Maybe you can see them once a month instead of once a week, or maybe you can make your visits shorter. And if you've built up so much anger toward them from bad past experiences that they usually bring out your worst side, you may need to stay away from them altogether. Some parents are so manipulative, so hard to stand up to, or so frustrating to be with, that any interaction with them isn't worth it.

Get Help If You Need It

If you can't work your way out of your routines, you may be in too deep. Perhaps you don't see where or how to cut back. Maybe you're having problems getting your message across to your folks. Possibly, your emotions are overwhelming you, and you're afraid of losing control.

In situations like these, you'd probably benefit from some outside help. For starters, you may want to find a good listener who's willing to be your sounding board. This can be a spouse, a sibling, or a friend. If you listen to your tone of voice as you speak to this person, you might get some clues about how you really feel. And sometimes, just the process of talking out loud can help you put things in perspective.

In addition to this, it might be a good idea to join a support group. It can be quite helpful to talk to others who are in the same situation that you're in. There are a number of places where support groups can be found. Some groups are oriented around particular medical problems, such as cancer, some are based in nursing homes for families with a relative in residence, and local adult education programs sometimes have classes for caregivers that can serve as support groups. When you talk about your problems with others who are having similar difficulties, you'll realize that you're not alone and that your feelings are shared by many. It will become clear to you that the parentcare years are a rough time for everyone.

Another option is to get professional counseling. Many people think that being in therapy is a sign of weakness and that anyone who sees a therapist must be incompetent or crazy. For many people it's less humiliating to see a physician for a physical problem than it is to work with a therapist in order to learn how to deal with the emotional issues that may be at the root of the physical problem. And then, some people resist paying good money for something that they can't be sure will help them.

But the truth is that psychotherapy can be a big help when you're stuck and unhappy. Even if you've been in therapy before and even if you believe that you've resolved the major issues that were complicating your relationship with your folks, you may still experience intense, difficult feelings as new situations come up. This is because the parent-child bond is always a highly-charged one.

There are many kinds of licensed therapists you can choose from, but all of them share the same general goals. They can help you become more aware of your feelings, they can help you break down your problems into smaller and more manageable parts, and they can help you act in your own best interest. Most people find the experience to be very supportive, even exhilarating. As you go through therapy, you can learn to think more clearly, take better charge of your life, and have more confidence in yourself and your decisions.

The trick is to find a good therapist who's suited to your own individual needs and style. To locate the right person, you may have to shop around. You can start by talking to people who've seen someone they've liked or by asking a trusted doctor for some recommendations. Cost shouldn't be a reason for not getting help because nearly every community has agencies that base their charges on a sliding fee scale, and some insurance policies include coverage for psychotherapy. If you truly want help, you can get it.

Take Good Care of Yourself

No matter how many demands your aging parents are putting on you, you should do everything you can to take good care of yourself. This means eating right, getting enough sleep and exercise, and maintaining your appearance. You should also allow ample time and energy for family and friends, for vacations (big and small), and for the little things you love to do like soaking in the tub, bringing home fresh flowers, taking a walk, or settling down with a good book. When you do these things, you'll be healthier and happier, and you'll have more vitality. You'll also be able to better enjoy being with your parent. It's your right and responsibility to take care of yourself. No one else is going to do it for you.

Feel Good About what You Are Doing

Remember that when you're helping your parents under difficult circumstances, you're entitled to feel good about the things that you're doing for them. If you focus on what you actually *are* doing instead of what you're not doing, you'll feel better about the situation.

Malcolm dutifully took his medication, and after a few days his physical symptoms improved. But it took him a bit longer to get into counseling. His wife nagged him for three weeks before he finally called a therapist from the list.

At first he was skeptical that therapy could do anything for him, but after a few visits he found that it actually felt good to talk to someone who was completely objective. It took him several weeks before he could acknowledge the anxiety, the frustration, the rage, the hurt, and the shame that he felt toward his mother. Eventually he was able to step back and see that he was never going to win her approval. He knew that he had to cut way back on his contact with her.

He and his wife mulled it over and decided that they'd do something twice a month with Samantha. They'd take her to church, to a movie, or to someplace else where conversation could be kept to a minimum. When she called him for help, Malcolm would suggest someone else who could handle the problem. He'd insist that she hire a financial manager. And when she criticized him, he would let her know how much it hurt him.

At first, it wasn't easy for Malcolm to be direct with his mother, but with the support of his wife and his therapist, he got better at it. Samantha had never heard him talk like this before, and she'd react by making a little joke or by trying to cajole him into doing what she wanted. But he usually held his ground. Once in a while he'd slip back into his old habits; but as his confidence increased, it happened less often.

So things improved, at least for Malcolm. Subsequent tests showed that his ulcer was healing, and he began to enjoy life more. Samantha, however, didn't change very much. Instead of calling her son for every little thing, she began depending on her new business manager.

Chapter

3

Getting Your Parents to Put Their Affairs in Order

Valerie's friend Edith was having a terrible year, and Valerie had suffered through it with her. Edith's elderly mother had been in a car accident and was completely incapacitated. She had to be fed through a tube, and she was totally unaware of her surroundings. Edith was distraught because there was no foreseeable end to the situation. She knew that her mother would never have wanted to be kept alive artificially like this. She was frustrated by the fact that she'd had to spend so much time and money with attorneys getting the power she needed to handle her mother's affairs. And she knew that her mother would never have wanted to sell her house and her beloved heirlooms in order to pay for her care. But there was nothing that Edith could do about all this.

Valerie was determined that such a thing would never happen to her widowed mother Emma. She wanted her mother to complete a few papers so that if she ever became incompetent, someone would be able to take care of her affairs and make critical *health decisions for her. But every time Valerie brought this up, her mother told her that she preferred not to talk about such morbid things.*

Some Concerns You May Have About Your Parents' Future

There are of a number of things you may be concerned about regarding your folks and the future. How are they going to manage when they become too frail to take care of themselves? If the time comes when they can't live independently, will they be able to afford to hire the help that they'll need? If they get sick, will they have enough insurance to take care of all of their medical expenses? Will they expect you to take care of them? Will they be able to go to a nice facility if they need to? And are their financial assets well enough protected so there might be something left over for you when they're gone?

Some people are natural planners and like to cover all of their bases. They feel more secure and in control of their lives if they make plans for the time when they won't be able to live independently. They're very careful with their money, and they try to invest it as best they can. They may take out additional insurance so that they'll be well covered, no matter what happens to them. And they may sell their home before they really need to so they can move into some sort of senior citizens' community or to a place that's closer to their children.

There are other people who aren't particularly interested in making arrangements for the future. They do their best to ignore the fact that the years are passing by, and they figure that they'll work things out if and when any difficulties come up. They may not have given much thought at all to financial planning. And they may be determined that they're going to live exactly where they want to—even if their choice is not a particularly practical one.

Most folks probably fall somewhere between these two extremes. They make certain provisions when it suits them, and they do their best to avoid making other kinds of arrangements that they'd prefer not to think about.

If your folks are lucky enough to have made profitable financial investments, they'll have more money to enjoy in their old age. If they've bought long-term care insurance and it turns out that one of them has to be institutionalized, the money that they've put into the premiums will have paid off. And if they've moved into a retirement community or to a place closer to you and end up happy with their decision, they'll have few regrets about giving up their house.

But these kinds of arrangements don't always work out so well. Investments don't always pay off, extra insurance benefits aren't always needed, and early moves sometimes turn out to be major disappointments.

In many ways, trying to plan for old age is a gamble. Most of the losses of aging are unpredictable, and there are so many different things that can go wrong. Sometimes people make unfortunate sacrifices long before they really need to.

If your folks feel happier and more secure because of certain arrangements that they've made for the future, then they're probably doing what's right for them. You can try to encourage them to do more if you don't believe they've done enough, but ultimately what they do is up to them. Everyone has different priorities, interests, and needs.

But there are two losses that everyone should prepare for—the certainty of death and the possibility of incompetence. Few people know when they're going to die, but everyone knows that it will happen eventually. And even though incompetence isn't inevitable, as death is, it is something that could happen to anyone at any time.

Your parents may believe that if they do nothing to prepare for these losses, they can magically hold off the day when such arrangements will be needed. They may prefer not to think about such unpleasant subjects. They may hate the idea of the paperwork that's involved. They may not want to spend the money on a lawyer. They may feel uneasy about giving someone else the power to pull the plug on them. Or they may simply want to avoid having to make difficult decisions. But if they die or become incompetent before they've put their affairs in order, there could be some very unfortunate consequences.

Once again, as Valerie was wrapping up a phone conversation with her mother, she tried to talk about making provisions for the possibility of her mother becoming incompetent. And once again, Emma told her that she'd prefer not to talk about such things.

Valerie informed Emma that she was becoming very annoyed with her foot-dragging. Then Emma informed Valerie that she was becoming even more annoyed with her nagging. She didn't think this kind of talk about being a vegetable was healthy at all.

Valerie told her mother that she was being totally unreasonable. Emma told her daughter that she was the one who was being unreasonable. Valerie raised her voice and said that some people were so stubborn and set in their ways that they needed to be nagged.

Then Emma hung up on her.

Valerie stared at the receiver. This was the first time she and her mother had had a fight since she was a teenager.

Putting Important Affairs in Order

Making Provisions for Death

First of all, each of your parents should write wills. Their wills should spell out how they want things distributed after they die. They can write the wills themselves, but these documents are important, so it's probably worthwhile for them to have an attorney help them. And your parents may want to talk to the attorney about establishing a trust. With a trust, estate taxes can sometimes be reduced. And with a living trust, there's the additional advantage that probate—an expensive, time-consuming, and completely public court proceeding—can be avoided.

If your parents die without wills, their assets will be distributed according to the laws of the state in which they live, and this may or may not be what they would have wanted. Furthermore, attorneys' fees and administrative costs could eat away a sizable chunk of their estate. And there could be considerable time delays as the probate court tries to assure that all assets have been found, that all debts are paid, and that all property is distributed to the proper heirs or beneficiaries.

When your parents prepare their will or trust, they'll name an executor or trustee who'll be the one to carry out their wishes. This person not only will need to know where to find the will or trust, but also will need to have access to a written inventory that specifies where all of their important papers are located. This would include bankbooks, insurance policies, stock certificates, bonds, and mortgages, as well as the location of safety deposit boxes and the keys to them. It can be both aggravating and time-consuming for survivors to have to search for these kinds of things, and sometimes valuable items are never located.

And finally, if your parents have definite preferences regarding burial or cremation or if they'd like a funeral or memorial service, they should discuss these things with their family members or, even better, they should write their wishes down. If one parent dies and you and the rest of your family have no guidelines to work with, you may end up agonizing over what kind of arrangements your parent would have wanted. Moreover, you may have to do all of this hastily and during a difficult time when you may not be able to think things out very clearly. As a consequence, you and your family members could end up squabbling among yourselves.

Making Provisions for Incompetence

As long as your parents are alert and able to make their own choices, they can handle their own business matters, or they can direct others to do it for them. And they can make health-care decisions for themselves as well. But problems will almost inevitably occur if they become incompetent—if they become demented or delirious, if they're in a coma, or if they're in any other condition that causes them to be unable to make reasonable decisions for themselves.

If your parents become incompetent without having made adequate arrangements, you may need to go to court to get conservatorship (called guardianship in some states) in order to take care of their business affairs. Conservatorship can involve a costly, time-consuming, and often emotionally difficult court proceeding. Because all family members must be notified that the proceeding is to take place, conflicts can come up if several relatives feel that they're the ones who should have the control. Then, once conservatorship is granted, there has to be an ongoing accounting to the court. And furthermore, the court must grant permission for any major changes that the conservator is considering.

To protect themselves and their loved ones from these kinds of problems, your parents should complete two documents while they're still competent. These documents are a Durable Power of Attorney for asset management and their state's preferred advanced medical directive.

A Durable Power of Attorney for asset management assigns an agent to handle someone's business affairs if that individual becomes incompetent. The specific name of the document will vary from state to state, but its purpose is the same throughout the country, and it's usually drawn up by an attorney. This shouldn't be confused with a general power of attorney, which designates someone to conduct business under an individual's direction. A general power of attorney remains valid only when someone is competent, and becomes invalid when he or she isn't able to make decisions.

The second document, an advanced medical directive, gives people some control over the aggressiveness with which they wish to be medically treated if they're no longer able to make their own decisions. (This is also a good place for people to designate in writing whether they'd prefer to be cremated or buried.) Each state has its own laws concerning the specific directive that it recognizes. Your parents' local hospital should have the proper form available, or the people there should know where the forms can be obtained. Your parents can use a standard form, or they can have an attorney draw one up if they want to make some special provisions.

The two most common advanced medical directives are the Living Will (also called Declaration to Physicians or Directive to Physicians) and the Durable Power of Attorney for Health Care. There are variations of the Living Will, but all of them basically stipulate that any treatment or procedure that merely prolongs dying must be withheld or withdrawn in the event of an incurable or irreversible condition. A Durable Power of Attorney for Health Care is different from a Living Will. The former designates a specific person to make health care decisions for an individual in the event that he or she can't do so. If your parents decide to complete either type of advanced medical directive, their personal physician must be willing to carry out their wishes and should be given a copy of the completed document as well.

There is a good reason why an advanced medical directive is necessary. Physicians are able to keep people alive who have virtually no quality of life. If your parents become incompetent and they haven't completed these forms, they could end up receiving aggressive medical treatment that you and your other family members are certain they never would have wanted. The emotional impact of this on families can be devastating, and the financial costs can be enormous. Furthermore, when people's lives are artificially prolonged, they suffer terribly and unnecessarily.

Valerie felt awful that she and her mother had gotten into a silly fight, and she decided to call her friend Edith to unload.

Edith didn't know what to say, but she suggested that Valerie come with her to the next meeting of her support group for children of aging parents.

Valerie decided to take her up on the idea. Maybe she'd learn something useful about how to handle her mother.

If you have questions, concerns, or suggestions regarding your folks' financial plans or life-style choices, you certainly can bring up the subject with them and see if they're interested in talking with you about these things. But when it comes to getting their affairs in order, you may want to give them a little shove.

The Bottom Line

If your folks make provisions for death and incompetence, both they and you will have greater peace of mind. Beyond that, any arrangements that they make for the future are strictly up to them.

How to Get Your Folks Moving

Be on the Lookout for Good Opportunities to Bring Up the Subject

It may be difficult for you to talk to your parents about getting their affairs in order. You may not like to think about the fact that they're going to die, and you may be afraid that they'll think you're being ghoulish or greedy for talking with them about these things.

To make it easier on yourself, it may help if you take advantage of the natural opportunities that come up. When there has been a death in the family or within their circle of friends, you can tactfully bring up the subject. When they're getting ready to go on a big trip, you can ask them if they've made provisions—just in case. When they're ill or if they've had an accident, you can try to initiate a frank talk. And when there has been a birth, a divorce, or a death in the family, you might mention to them that this may be a good time to make some arrangements or to revise any arrangements that they've already made. During such times, your parents may be more inclined to think about their own mortality.

These matters can be touchy, and you'll need to be as diplomatic as you can. And especially if you have your own life in tip-top order and your parents don't, you may have a hard time dealing with the fact that their style is different from yours.

If Your Parents Bring Up the Subject Themselves, By All Means Let Them Talk

Your parents may be matter-of-fact about the subject, and you may be the one who's uncomfortable talking about these things. Consequently, you may be tempted to cut them off when they start to tell you about the arrangements they've made or they're thinking about making.

You should try not to do this. They may sense your discomfort, and it may be difficult for them to bring the subject up again.

Put Your Own Affairs in Order and Tell Your Parents About It

One very important thing that you can do is to put your own affairs in order. Then you can share the fact that you've done so with your parents, and you can encourage them to do the same for themselves. You may have discovered that there have been recent changes in the tax laws, and this could give you a good excuse to bring up the subject with them. Or you may find that after you've been through the process yourself, you're more sensitive to the issues that are fueling their resistance, and it might help matters if they see that these kinds of arrangements aren't only for people who are old or sick. Besides, you should put your own affairs in order anyway.

If You Feel Uncomfortable Bringing Up the Subject, Ask a Trusted Intermediary to Speak With Your Parents

You may feel less awkward if you discuss the matter first with the parent who's easier for you to talk with. If you think that your folks might be more responsive to someone other than you, you can ask another family member or a close friend of theirs to bring up the subject with them. Perhaps someone nearer to their age will have better luck than you'll have. Or perhaps they'll be convinced by others who have had an unfortunate experience themselves.

Be Sure That Your Parents Get Any Assistance That They Need

It might help to get things moving if you give your folks a magazine article or a basic book on estate planning. And, you can offer to help them out with any specific tasks that may be giving them trouble. If they haven't made a written inventory because they find the idea of organizing their papers too overwhelming, you can offer to help them with the job; you can suggest that they hire someone to help them.

Encourage Your Parents to Hire an Attorney

Your parents should use a lawyer who specializes in estate planning. In order to find a good attorney, they can get recommendations from other people they know.

Even though you may be tempted to find a lawyer for them, it's important that they get their own. If you (or anyone else) contact the attorney or pay the legal fees, the question of undue influence could be raised later.

If Your Parents are Still Not Putting Their Affairs in Order, Drop the Subject for Now

People's attitudes are often slow to change, and it may take years before your parents are willing to think about these issues, so try not to make a pest of yourself. As time goes by, they may come around.

In the meantime, if they choose not to listen to your well-intentioned advice, remember that it's their right to live their lives as they see fit. It's certainly not worth it for you to ruin your relationship with them over this.

There were eight other women at Edith's support group meeting. Some of them had been coming for quite some time. Valerie could see that most of the others had problems that were far worse than her own, and she doubted that she'd want to attend more than one session. She was a little nervous, but she figured that she might as well plunge right in and tell the group about her situation.

After she shared her problem, the others told her about similar experiences of their own, and soon she began to see that she was trying to control her mother too much. Valerie felt a little defensive about this at first, but because the others freely admitted that they were often guilty of the very same thing, she didn't feel so bad. She realized that it might be best if she backed off.

The next day, Valerie drove to her mother's place. She told Emma about the meeting, apologized for being so bossy, and said she wouldn't bug her anymore. Her mother happily accepted her daughter's apology and said she was sorry for hanging up on her.

Later, when Valerie was leaving, Emma mentioned that she'd been thinking about it and wondered if it might be possible for Valerie to take her to the nursing home to see Edith's mother.

Valerie smiled to herself and said that she'd be happy to take her anytime.

Chapter 4

Taking Things One Small Step at a Time

Molly was a cello teacher who lived with her engineer husband in the suburbs. Their children were away at college. Molly's eighty-two-year-old father Chester was a long-time widower who lived with his sister in the city. Because Chester didn't even know how to boil water, no one liked to think about what would happen if his sister died first. So when she did, Molly and her brother and sister had no idea about what to do with their father. The only thing they could think of was to have him move in with one of them.

But there were problems with this plan. Molly's brother lived right there in the city, but he spent long hours at his dry cleaning business, and the condo he shared with his wife was too small for another person. Molly's sister was divorced and had the space, but she lived hours away and traveled much of the time on business. Molly had the extra room and was home much of the time, but she taught students in her living room, and she knew how much her husband enjoyed his privacy.

She was very surprised when her husband suggested that Chester move in with them. Although she had her misgivings, she couldn't think of a better alternative, so she agreed to give it a try.

So her father gave up his apartment, got rid of most of his belongings, and moved in with Molly.

When You're Tempted to Go Overboard

When your parents begin to have significant problems, you may panic and not know which way to turn as you search for answers. Because you can't be aware of all the possible options, your first impulse may be to resort to an extreme solution. You may hope that by making a sweeping change, you'll be able to take care of not only the current problem but also any future problems that might come up as well.

But there are drawbacks to this approach. A major change can cause your parents to become prematurely dependent on other people, and it can prevent them from functioning at their highest potential. Furthermore, their self-esteem may suffer because they won't be doing what they can for themselves.

The Bottom Line

Your folks will remain independent longer, and they'll probably feel better about themselves, if they take things one Small Step at a time.

A Small Step is an incremental adjustment to the immediate problem at hand. It's a change that's appropriate and necessary under the circumstances, and ideally it's one that's as nondisruptive as possible. For any given problem, there are often several potential solutions.

For example, if your dad is having trouble managing some everyday chores such as shopping or meal preparation, there are a number of Small Steps that he can take.

If getting to the store is the problem, all he may need to do is find some form of transportation. He can get rides with friends, hire a driver, take a bus or a cab, or sign up for a senior citizens' shopping van service.

If shopping has become too difficult for him, he may be able to prepare his own meals if someone shops for him. Or he can order his food from a market that delivers.

If he has trouble preparing his own meals but he'd like to continue doing his own cooking, he may be able to do it if he makes a few changes. He can organize his kitchen so everything is stored on low shelves. Or he can use adaptive equipment to manage tasks such as opening jars or turning faucets on and off.

If there's no way that he can prepare his own meals, or if he doesn't particularly want to cook, he could share his home with a friend or a relative who's willing. Or he could arrange for someone to help him with his shopping and cooking in exchange for room and board. He could also have his midday meal at a local senior center, or he could have it delivered to his home through a meal delivery program. And in addition, he could use frozen meals that are ready to pop into the microwave oven, or he could work out an arrangement with a restaurant that delivers. He also could hire someone to come in to cook his meals for him a few times a week, and then he could reheat the meals later. Or, if he can afford it, he could hire full-time, live-in help.

Some Small Steps Along the Way

There are many steps that can be taken for just about any problem. The trick is to figure out what the problem is and then to settle on a reasonable solution. Here are some things your parents can do to optimize their independence and their sense of well-being.

Safety Tips

Safety, of course, should always come first. Accident prevention is one of the best ways to avoid problems and to help people stay independent. These safety tips are particularly applicable for older people:

- Throw rugs should be removed or else they should have nonskid backing on them so your parents won't trip on them.

- Uncarpeted floors shouldn't be slippery. A high-gloss polish should not be used.

- Nonskid strips should be placed on uncarpeted stairs and in the tub and shower.

- If necessary, additional phones should be installed for quick access and to prevent tripping over cords.

- Emergency phone numbers should be clearly posted near all phones.

- Smoke detectors should be installed near the kitchen and all bedrooms, and checked regularly.

- A fire extinguisher should be in the kitchen. Your parents should know how to use it, and be capable of doing so if necessary.

- They should know the best way out of their house or apartment building in case of fire.

- All steps, stairs, and banisters should be in good repair.

- All windows and doors should be easily locked and unlocked.

- Electric cords should be in good shape, and kept well out of the way of foot traffic.

- All appliances should be in good working condition.

- Hot and cold water faucets should be clearly marked.

- The hot water heater temperature should be set below the scalding point.

- Furnaces and exhaust systems should be checked regularly, and filters should be replaced when necessary.

- All areas of the home, both inside and out, should be well lit, especially stairs. In addition, night lights should be used in the bedroom, hall, and bathroom.

- It takes longer for the eyes of elderly people to adapt when they move from light to dark areas, so solitary bright lights should be replaced by several more diffuse lights. Also, highly reflective surfaces should be eliminated because the lenses of many older people's eyes become cloudy, and as a result, the glare that bounces off shiny surfaces can confuse them.

- To absorb noises and echoes that can bother hard-of-hearing people, carpeting and curtains can be installed.

Special Equipment

Adaptive equipment can make almost any task easier or safer for disabled people. There are hundreds of different items that are available at hospital supply stores and through specialty catalogs that feature assistive devices and sick-room equipment. It's usually a good idea, however, to get some help from an occupational therapist or a physical therapist when you're ordering special equipment. They'll know how to help your parent select the most appropriate item and how to customize it if necessary. Here's a sampling of some of the items that are available:

- Clothes that open in the front make it possible for people with limited use of their arms to dress themselves.

- A button loop is very useful for one-hand buttoning.

- Specially designed utensils allow people with such problems as arthritis, tremors, limited range of motion, and weakness to perform all sorts of tasks from gardening to putting on makeup.

- Raised toilet seats make toileting easier for people who have difficulty getting up from a sitting position.

- Hand-held shower heads and bath benches make it possible for people who can't stand up in the shower to bathe themselves.

- Flexible foot dressers make it easier for people who can't bend over to put on socks and hose.

- Intercoms make it possible to hear another person in another room.

Help at Home

Another good way to solve certain kinds of problems is to hire help. However, finding and keeping dependable, qualified, reasonably priced help isn't always easy. And turnover can sometimes be an annoyance. People who are successful at keeping good help make it a practice to clearly explain to their employees what is expected of them. They also treat them respectfully, give them regular raises, and know how to express their appreciation for a job well done.

Your parents can find help themselves, or they can find someone through an agency. If they hire help on their own, they'll probably pay less, they can personally select the person they hire, and they'll have more flexibility in scheduling. But they may need to spend extra time, money, and effort in advertising, interviewing, and selecting the person. And in addition to these things, the person they hire won't be insured, they'll have to do all the supervising themselves, and they won't have any coverage for absenteeism unless they work out some sort of special arrangement with the employee.

If your parents go through an agency, the employee will be screened, licensed, bonded, insured, and supervised. And furthermore, help will be available twenty-four hours a day, seven days a week; back-ups will be obtainable if necessary. But this will probably cost more, they may not always be able to personally select the employee themselves, and different helpers may come in on different days.

The best way for your parents to find help outside of an agency is to ask friends and acquaintances if they know someone who's looking for work. They can also place ads in newsletters or post notices on bulletin boards of churches, synagogues, or other organizations to which they belong. If this fails, they can answer ads in the paper, put an ad in the paper themselves, check with placement offices in local colleges, or see if a local hospital or organization that works with the elderly or disabled has listings of people who are available to hire. They can save some money if they offer room and board in exchange for at least part of the helper's salary.

Special Programs and Services

In many communities there are dozens of locally-based resources that can help your parents live as safely and independently as they can.

- Postal alert programs arrange for letter carriers to call a designated person if the carriers see trouble signs at the homes of registered participants. A special decal inside the mailbox indicates that a person has registered for the program.

- Telephone reassurance services are staffed by volunteers who make daily phone calls to check on people who are isolated in their homes.

- Personal emergency response systems allow people to summon help when they can't get to a phone. If they activate an electronic device that is worn around the neck, the service will contact a designated person. Some systems also can alert the police, the paramedics, and the fire department.

- Handicapped-accessible transportation services use specially equipped vans or buses to give rides to people who have difficulty using public transportation.

- Friendly visitor and adopt-a-grandparent programs send

out volunteer visitors every week to spend some time with shut-ins.

- Share-a-home programs match up people who have extra space in their homes with others who need living quarters.

- Senior day-care programs offer socialization opportunities and other activities for the frail elderly. They also provide caregivers with some time off.

- Library volunteers deliver and pick up books for people who can't get out easily.

- Counselor-teachers for the blind are available through state rehabilitation departments. They teach daily living skills (often in the home) to people who are losing or who have already lost their eyesight.

- Talking Books can be used by the sight-impaired and by those who are unable to hold books or turn pages. The machines and the tapes are sometimes available at public libraries or at service organizations for the blind. People can get additional tapes through the mail from the Library of Congress and its branch offices.

- Home health agencies provide skilled nursing care; social services; physical, occupational, and speech therapy; and personal care assistance for homebound people who are under a doctor's care for a new or a worsening medical problem.

- Some physicians operate out of vans rather than out of offices. They provide primary care medical services in people's homes for those who can't get out easily.

- There are dozens of national associations such as the Alzheimer's Association and the Arthritis Foundation that have branch offices in local communities. They provide current information and can refer people to special services that are available.

- Some communities have medical equipment loan closets that stock everything from bedpans to hospital beds.

Financial Strategies

There are quite a few options your parents can take advantage of that will help their money go farther.

- Certified financial planners, tax accountants, and estate planning or tax attorneys can tell them about investment opportunities, life insurance trusts, charitable deductions, and other income and estate planning strategies that can make their money work better for them.

- If your parents own their home and they need to supplement their income, there are a variety of home equity conversion programs for which they may be eligible. They can learn about the programs that are available in their state by contacting the National Center for Home Equity Conversion.

Financial Assistance

If money is a problem for your parents, there are some steps they can take that will help them with their expenses.

- Subsidized rental housing for eligible low-income elderly people is available through local housing authorities.

- Utility companies sometimes offer discounts to people who are on limited incomes.

- Some communities have funds that have been earmarked for special purposes, such as helping people with extraordinary medical expenses, providing respite help for caregivers, and purchasing special pieces of equipment that aren't covered by insurance.

- Health fairs provide free diagnostic medical screening.

- Some physicians will accept Medicare payments as payment in full when they know that a person is having financial difficulties.

- Some nonprofit or county health care providers offer health services on a sliding fee basis.

- People who were honorably discharged from wartime service and who meet certain specific criteria for disability and financial need, may be eligible for a Non Service-Connected Pension with Aide and Attendance through the Veteran's Administration.

- When people have a monthly income that's at the poverty level and when most of their assets have been used up, they may be eligible for Supplemental Security Insurance (SSI) through the Social Security Office. This will give them additional monthly income and will provide them with Medicaid coverage for many of the medical expenses that Medicare doesn't cover. It also provides payment for in-home or institutional care if this becomes necessary. Even if their monthly income is too high for SSI, they may be eligible for some of these benefits through their state public assistance office.

- If one of your parents needs to be in a nursing home, there's the risk that all of their assets will be used up in order to pay for the care of the one who's institutionalized. To prevent this from happening, a portion of their assets and income (including their home) can be excluded in determining the institutionalized parent's eligibility for Medicaid. This way, the parent who's in the nursing home can become eligible for help without impoverishing your other parent.

Applying for public assistance is time-consuming and requires patience. Furthermore, not all doctors and nursing homes will accept Medicaid payments, and certain medications may not be covered.

And then there's the fact that some people are reluctant to accept public assistance. They may have always paid their own way and feel humiliated that they must now accept charity. If your parents have this attitude, they may need to be reminded that they've worked hard and paid taxes for years and that now it's their turn to get some help.

Moving

There may come the time when your parents will have to think seriously about moving from their home because it has become too inconvenient, too unsafe, or too lonely for them to live there anymore. Here again, there are many options that are available to them. Some of these choices will allow them to maintain their independence and privacy longer than they might otherwise be able to.

Most of the time, it's a good idea for older people to stay in the area in which they already live so that their social relationships are disrupted as little as possible, but many people move to new communities and end up being happy with their decision. If your parents are thinking of moving to a new community, they should consider trying the move out on a trial basis before they make it permanent.

It's important to keep in mind that moving is rarely easy for older people. They almost always go through a difficult adjustment period as they get used to new faces, the new routines, and the new physical environment. The adjustment can take months.

They can move to a smaller place. They could buy or rent a smaller house or a condominium, rent an apartment, or purchase a mobile home. And, if they choose, they can move into a retirement community that has been designed for people over the age of fifty-five.

They can move to your community in order to be closer to you. This can work out fine, but you and your parents would be well-advised to consider the move carefully. You may think that your parents' problems will be solved if they live near you, but it doesn't always happen that way.

They could live under the same roof with you. This is an arrangement that has a number of possible variations. They could move into an extra room in your home. A space in your home could be converted into living quarters for them. Rooms could be added to your home so that they'd have their own separate living space. You could move in with them. They could take turns living with you and your siblings. Or all of you could pool your resources and move into a larger home together.

For some families, any of these variations would be out of the question. For others, living together under the same roof could work out very well. But even under the best of circumstances, when an elderly parent and an adult child live together, there's plenty of potential for problems. Each member of the household has to make significant adjustments, and issues such as privacy, the allocation of space, and the distribution of responsibilities have to be dealt with. Furthermore, any solutions that have been hammered out will probably have to be re-evaluated as the older person's needs change.

However, the touchiest thing about this arrangement is the fact that dormant emotional issues between parents and adult children can become re-ignited when the two generations live in close proximity.

For all of these reasons, this is an option that should be thought out carefully and handled sensitively if you decide to give it a try.

They could move into a group living situation. Some people don't like the idea of group living because they don't want to give up their privacy and their independence. Others see it as an opportunity to be liberated from unwanted responsibilities. Your parents' needs and interests as well as their physical capabilities and their financial situation will determine which of the different group living options are possible for them.

- Retirement hotels usually provide meals and a weekly cleaning service along with a room or a suite of rooms and a bathroom. They don't have any special licensing, so residents are expected to be able to walk unassisted and to manage all of their own care. Many retirement hotels offer activity programs for seniors who enjoy being with others.

- Residential care homes (also called board and care homes) are licensed and regulated facilities that range in size from small, privately owned homes that can accommodate one or two elderly people to large institutional complexes that can house hundreds of residents. Residential care homes provide room and board along with various levels of personal assistance. Occasionally, retirement hotels and apartment buildings for seniors offer a certain number of assisted-living units.

- Skilled nursing facilities (also known as nursing homes, convalescent homes, extended care facilities, and health care facilities), provide round-the-clock skilled nursing care as well as personal care. The atmosphere in a skilled nursing facility is almost always more hospital-like than home-like, and most of the residents are either quite disabled or demented.

- Continuing care communities consist of apartments or cottages that are located on the same premises with assisted-living units and a skilled nursing facility. Most residents start off living independently in their own small apartments. Later on if they need it, they can move into one of the other facilities where they'll receive more care. These communities often have strict rules in regard to age, finances, and health status upon entry; and they usually have what's called a buy-in feature whereby new residents must pay a substantial nonrefundable deposit. Residents also pay a monthly fee, which varies according to the size of their living quarters and the level of care that they require. The one big advantage of continuing care communities over other group living situations is the fact that they provide all of the care that residents will need for the rest of their lives no matter what their condition might be.

It wasn't long before Molly and her husband realized that they'd made a big mistake. They missed their privacy, and Chester's presence was more of a disruption than they'd anticipated.

The constant blaring of sports events on the television drove Molly nuts. She became unnerved when her father would wander in and out of the living room while she was trying to teach or practice. And she'd grit her teeth when he constantly followed her around chatting. And things weren't much better for her husband. When he got home from work, he enjoyed playing with his computer. But no matter how engrossed he was, his father-in-law wouldn't hesitate to come into his study looking for companionship.

Late one night, Molly and her husband were in the kitchen and got into a rather loud discussion about what to do about her dad. Then, Chester walked into the room.

Molly was embarrassed that her father had heard them, but Chester didn't seem to be upset at all. In fact, he joined right in and told them that he was unhappy with the arrangement too. He hated the suburbs and was homesick for the city. He'd wanted to tell them earlier but hadn't wanted to hurt their feelings.

All three of them felt much better once the truth was out in the open, and they agreed that Chester needed to find somewhere else to live.

But where?

There will be times when the solution to a particular problem is obvious. When your dad needs to get an amplifier for his phone, he can probably figure out what to do all by himself, or you can help him figure it out.

And there will be other times when someone else will give him the information he needs. A bus driver who sees that he has difficulty getting onto the bus may tell him about handicapped transportation services that the bus company offers.

But other times, the answers will be more difficult to come by.

How to Scout Out the Best Small Step

Track Down a Pro Who Knows the Ropes

It's certainly possible to do your own research and to dig up solutions on your own, but you'll make things much easier for yourself if you get some help from a Pro Who Knows the Ropes—someone who works in geriatrics, is up to date on all the resources in the community, and can give you expert advice. Most Pros are social workers, nurses, or gerontologists; but they can be members of other professions as well.

They can assist you in figuring out exactly what the problem is, sorting out the options, mapping out a plan, and getting the momentum going. They can guide you through the maze of senior services in your parents' area, and can provide you with customized referrals. Then, if you run into any rough spots or dead ends, they can help you get back on track and can give you emotional support that will help you feel more confident about your decision and less guilty about what you're doing.

Consulting with Pros is much like seeing a lawyer or a doctor. You present a full and honest account of the problem, and they give you the best advice that they can. You may need to speak to them only once. Or you may have to get together several times with them until the situation is resolved.

Sometimes an expert will practically fall into your lap. If your parent is in the hospital, for example, you may receive a call from someone from the Social Service Department asking you to take part in a discharge planning meeting with your parent. But there will be other times when you'll need to look for one.

The best way to start looking is to call the area Agency on Aging in your parents' community. If they can't help you, they should be able to refer you to another agency that can. They may suggest that you call the geriatric assessment team at the local health department. They may connect you with a geriatric care manager on the staff of a social service agency such as the Family Service Agency, Catholic Social Service, or Jewish Family Service. If your parent is receiving care from a home health agency or a hospice organization, they may direct you to the social worker on its staff. If your parent needs to relocate to a licensed group living facility, they may recommend that you call the Long-Term Care Ombudsman for guidance. Or if your parent has a particular medical problem, they may advise you to call the local chapter of the national organization that concerns itself with that condition.

Another thing you can do is hire a private geriatric care manager who works in your parents' community. These people are in private practice and charge an hourly fee for their services. They can be especially valuable if you live far away from your parents and can't do much of the footwork yourself. This profession is new and largely unregulated, so it's a good idea to check people's references carefully and to make certain that you're hiring an experienced person. The National Association of Private Geriatric Care Managers issues a registry of its certified members.

Involve Your Parents in the Decision-making Process

It's important that your folks be as involved as possible in solving their own problems. After all, they're the ones who'll be the most affected by any decisions. Even if they're demented, even if they don't seem to understand what's happening to them, and even if they don't care what's decided (or say that they don't), they should still be involved. The more they participate, the better the chances are that they'll cooperate in carrying out whatever decision is made.

When your folks are competent, they should be totally involved in making any decisions. When they're less competent, you can give them two or three choices and ask them to give you their input. And when they're unable to participate at all, you can still tell them what the family is considering; later on, tell them what has been decided. You can do this even when you're not sure if they understand you.

If Your Parent is Indecisive, Start Things Moving a Bit

Sometimes people who are perfectly capable of making decisions will hesitate to do so because it's so hard for them to make changes. With these kinds of people, it may help if you take the first step and get the ball rolling for them. Your father may like the idea of sharing his home, but he may put off the process of going forward with it because he finds the idea of selecting the right person to be overwhelming. If you do some of the groundwork for him and start the momentum going, he may be happy to proceed once he sees that the task isn't as difficult as he imagined.

If the Decision is a Big One, Hold a Family Conference

When a significant change must be made, a family conference may be in order. Such a meeting is most effective if it's held immediately after a major crisis has occurred because this is a time when everyone knows that a decision is necessary and when everyone will be most likely to make the effort to participate.

The entire family should be invited to the conference, particularly those who'll be directly affected by the decision. Grandchildren and friends of your folks can be involved too, if the decision will have an impact on them. Those who can't be there in person can participate via a telephone conference call. And of course your parents should be present.

Ideally, the meeting should be led by a Pro. If an impartial person is in charge, the others will be on their best behavior, and the discussion will stay more focused. A leader can also offer useful ideas and can answer questions that come up.

Settle on the Best Small Step

Whether or not there's a family conference, it may not be easy for you and your parents to find a truly happy solution for a particular problem. Making decisions can be tough even under the best of circumstances, but when none of the choices are good, it can be downright grim. It can be especially frustrating when there are many unknown factors. You have no idea how much longer your dad will live. You don't know for sure if his money will last long enough. You can't know whether he'll improve or deteriorate. And when decisions have to be made quickly, the situation will be even more stressful.

You may be a person who decides things by listening to your heart and plunging right in. Or you may be one who uses your head and carefully weighs every choice you make. If you want to help your folks, you'll have to listen to both your head and your heart. You'll need to analyze the options, but you'll also need to trust your instincts.

- Try to imagine yourself living out the various scenarios. Think about what it would be like to visit your dad in a nursing home.

- Talk to others who have been in similar situations. When your neighbor's mom was in a nursing home, did she eventually adjust?

- Get more facts if you need to. Once you know the current value of your dad's house, both of you may change your minds about selling it.

- Listen to your tone of voice and pay attention to your body language. If you notice that your throat tightens up when you tell your dad that you'd be happy to do his laundry every week, you may want to think more carefully about what you're getting yourself into.

- If you're stuck and can't settle on a solution, a Pro or a counselor may be able to help.

Keep in Mind that Few Decisions Have to be Permanent and that There's No Shame in Changing Your Mind

With time, it may become obvious that the decision that was made wasn't the right one. If this happens, you should remember that there's nothing wrong with trying something different. You did the best you could with the information that you had at the time.

Molly called around and talked with some of her friends who had elderly parents to see if any of them had any ideas for her, and she visited several local nursing homes. But nothing seemed right. Then she asked her brother to check out Chester's old neighborhood.

He couldn't find anything, but he did get the number of the local Ombudsman Office from one of the nursing homes that he'd visited. Molly called the office and made an appointment for herself and her brother to come and talk.

They had a long, fruitful discussion with the director, and it became clear to them that what they were looking for was a retirement hotel. The director gave them a list of five places that would be appropriate for Chester.

Molly and her brother took their dad to visit them. None of the hotels were absolutely wonderful, but one stood out because the large lobby had a homey feeling and because it was located near a park. Chester would have to take two buses to see his friends in his old neighborhood, but it was within walking distance of his son's business.

Unfortunately, it didn't have any vacancies.

Getting Through the Glitches, the Hassles, and the Runaround

Once you and your folks have settled on the best Small Step you can find, there may still be some logistical hurdles to get over. You may have trouble nailing down certain details. You may not be able to connect with some of the available services. And you may run into red tape. These kinds of problems can be annoying, but they shouldn't prevent you from getting what you need.

As a general rule, you should use the phone as much as possible. You may prefer to do things in person (and there will be times when this really is best), but most of the time it will be in your best interest to save time and gas by using the phone. If you don't feel comfortable talking on the phone, see if you can find someone who's willing to help you with this task. (This might be a good job for your brother or sister.)

Take good notes as you gather information, and jot down the date and time of each call along with the name of each person you speak to. Try to be assertive, but also try to be as diplomatic as possible. If you don't understand something, say so. If one person can't help you, ask for the name of someone else who may be able to. And you might want to follow up on your calls to make certain that the situation is being taken care of.

If you're having difficulty getting results, a good way to have an impact on people is to share your feelings with them. You can explain how frustrated, worried, and scared you are. And you can ask them to suggest how you can be better at getting what you need. If you're still not getting any satisfaction, you can ask to speak to a supervisor. With your written record at hand, you should be able to go over the steps that you've already taken.

Try not to take rudeness, incompetence, or inefficiency personally. If one particular individual is brusque, you may be able to achieve a better rapport if you tell the person that you understand how tough that job must be.

And finally, if you need to go to an office in order to fill out an application, be sure to find out ahead of time which specific documents you'll need to bring along. You can also ask how much time will probably be involved, and you can make your appointment for a time when the office is least busy. If you know that you may have a long wait, you might bring something to do.

Because Chester liked this one particular retirement hotel so much, Molly asked around and finally found a gentleman who was willing to have a roommate. She arranged things so that when a single room became available, Chester would have have a chance at it. Her dad wasn't crazy about the idea of sharing a room, but since none of the other places appealed to him, he decided to go ahead with the move.

In the beginning, he was at loose ends. He had a hard time getting used to his roommate's snoring, he wasn't all that fond of the food, and it was too time-consuming and tiring for him to take the two buses across town very often to see his old friends. Because he had nothing better to do, he began hanging out at his son's dry cleaning store.

At first, his son didn't want his dad to be there because he thought that he'd get in the way. But Chester loved gabbing with the customers, he was good at retrieving the cleaned clothes, and he freed up his son to supervise the help. Pretty soon, Chester became a regular, and his son came to appreciate his assistance.

Slowly, Chester got more accustomed to life in the retirement hotel. He found a friend who liked to play checkers. After several months, he was still waiting for a single room, but he had to admit that he was much happier than when he was at Molly's.

And so was she.

Part II

The Complications

Chapter 5

When You're Not Sure If You Should Step In

Doug's parents were in their late sixties and had always been quiet, private people. They'd never given Doug much cause to worry about them, but during the past several months, Doug and his wife had become concerned about his father, Charles. Charles hadn't been particularly happy since he'd retired a few years earlier from his job as a press operator with the local newspaper. But lately he'd become quite moody, and it seemed that he rarely went out of the house.

However, because his father appeared to be doing well in every other way, Doug figured that he was probably just being crotchety because he was getting old. And because Doug didn't want to make a big deal out of nothing, he kept quiet and minded his own business.

When the Situation Is Iffy

When your folks get into their later years and begin to experience some of the losses of aging, your first hint of trouble may not come from a phone call informing you that something awful has happened. Instead, you gradually may become suspicious that things aren't exactly as they should be. It may be that something bothers you about your parents' appearance. Or there may be something about their behavior that has changed. Or they may have made a decision that makes you wonder about their judgment or their competence.

Does your dad's coughing mean that he's coming down with a serious illness? Does the fact that his hands shake affect his life in any significant way? Does he even notice the shaking? Does this once impeccable man realize that he has stains on his clothes and that he looks unkempt?

You don't know if these things are serious or not, and you can't help but feel a little worried.

One Sunday, after Doug and his family had finished eating dinner at his folks' house, Charles went down to his basement woodworking shop while the others sat down to visit in the living room.

A few moments later, they heard a series of thuds coming from the direction of the basement.

They ran to see what had happened and found Charles lying at the bottom of the stairs. He'd cut his head and was dazed.

They were frightened because there was a great deal of blood, so Doug wrapped his father's head in a towel, and he and his mother took him to the emergency room.

Some Red Flags

There are dozens of possible signs that can indicate that your folks may have a problem that's worth looking into. Any of these Red Flags should put you on the alert.

- Your dad has gained or lost a great deal of weight.

- He's eating more than usual but isn't gaining weight.

- He's drinking a great deal of water.

- He's wearing excessive or insufficient clothing.

- He's unkempt, he doesn't smell clean, or he has stains on his clothes.

- He has bruises, burns, or other signs of injuries on his body.

- He scratches himself a lot.

- He has an unusual growth on his skin.

- His skin color isn't normal.

- The whites of his eyes look bloodshot or discolored.

- He squints when he's reading, or he holds reading matter either very close to his face or very far away.

- He bumps into things.

- He speaks too loudly or softly. He asks others to repeat what they've said. He keeps the TV or radio on very loud. He turns his head toward whomever he's talking to. He cups his hand to his ear when others are talking to him. Or he accuses others of mumbling or talking too fast.

- He coughs a great deal or is short of breath.

- He sleeps propped up with several pillows.

- He seems tired much of the time.

- He sleeps more than usual during the day.

- He moves more slowly than normal.

- His driving isn't safe.

- He has difficulty getting up from chairs.

- He limps when he walks.

- His feet or legs are swollen.

- He often loses his balance.

- He makes frequent trips to the bathroom.

- He isn't paying his bills, or he's paying the same bills more than once.

- He doesn't seem to be interested in much of anything.

- He acts nervous or distracted.

- He's more antisocial or reclusive than usual.

- He's forgetful, he seems confused much of the time, or he leaves things in odd places around the house.

- When you ask him questions, he gives you a vague or an incomplete answer.

- He talks about feeling hopeless or about ending his life.

- He has unusual mood swings.

- He's reluctant to leave home, he's excessively worried about small things, or he's preoccupied with his health.

- He has allowed his home and yard to fall into poor repair.

Red Flags are indications that something might be wrong when they signal a change from the way that things have been in the past. Your dad may never have been a great driver, but if he has been in more than a few fender benders lately, you may now wonder if he should be driving at all. He may never have been particularly quick on his feet because of his weight, but if he has been short of breath recently after only walking up the front steps, you may worry that he could be ripe for a heart attack. He may never have been much of a talker, but if he's barely speaking at all, you may be concerned that he could have something wrong with his mind.

In the emergency room, the doctor who was on duty that evening examined Charles, sutured his head wound, and sent him for an X ray. Then she took Doug and his mother aside and told them that she'd smelled alcohol on Charles' breath and had ordered some blood tests. She asked them if he had a drinking problem.

They were a little taken aback by her question and told her that Charles usually did have a few gin-and-tonics before dinner. But they said they seriously doubted that he had a drinking problem.

The doctor accepted their assessment and said that she wanted to keep Charles in the hospital under observation overnight in case he showed any signs of head injury. Doug and his mother agreed to go along with whatever she thought was best.

Doug wondered to himself if it was possible that his father could have a drinking problem that they didn't know about. If he did, it certainly would explain a lot of things.

When You Hesitate to Step Forward

There may be times when you'll notice something that concerns you about your parents, but you don't feel comfortable saying anything about it. If you can see that your dad is having difficulty reading small print, you may feel awkward pointing this out to him because you know that he doesn't like to think about the fact that he's getting older. You don't want to humiliate him or upset him, and because he hasn't complained about anything or asked you for any advice, you may be afraid that you'd be overstepping your bounds if you said something.

And there are other factors that can figure into the equation as well. It may be painful for you to acknowledge that your parents aren't the capable people that they used to be, and because you don't like to see them deteriorate, you may prefer to look the other way. Or you may know that something isn't quite right with them, but you may not be able to put your finger on exactly what it is. Or the situation may not seem particularly serious, so you may decide to let it ride because you don't have the time or the energy to get involved at the moment. Or you may figure that the changes that you're seeing are simply the inevitable signs of the aging process and that there's nothing that can be done about them anyway. Or you may sense that your folks are trying to hide their problems and that they don't want to talk about them. Or you may have already mentioned other similar concerns once or twice to your parents, and they may not have been very receptive to you.

Your hesitation to get involved has much to do with the kind of relationship that you have with your parents and also with the kind of people that both of you are. Some parents and children are very direct and forthright with each other, and others have more reserved relationships.

But despite all of the reasons why you may prefer to keep your concerns to yourself, you should give your parents the benefit of the doubt and speak up. They may surprise you, and they may be willing to talk frankly with you. And if not, at least you'll feel better for having expressed yourself, and you won't go around agonizing about whether or not you should say something to them.

There are many good reasons why you should try to be straightforward with your parents. For one thing, many problems have simple solutions that can be corrected easily. If your dad is losing a lot of weight for no apparent reason, the problem may only be that his dentures aren't fitting properly and that he's eating less because of this. And for another thing, it's almost always better to get problems taken care of early on before they get worse. If you notice that your dad is drinking a lot of water and is going to the bathroom more than usual, it's a good idea to get him to a doctor. If it turns out that he has developed diabetes, he can get on a proper diet right away, and he may be able to avoid becoming dependent on insulin. And finally, you may find out that what looks like a problem isn't one after all. If you mention to your dad that he seems to be going to the bathroom a lot, you may find out that he's doing this because he's on a new medication.

The Bottom Line

When something is bothering you and you're genuinely concerned about your folks, the time to get involved is now.

How to Get Into the Act Without Overstepping Your Bounds

Ask Other People for Their Impressions of What's Going On

When it's not clear to you if what you're seeing is a problem or not, you can speak with your spouse, your other parent, your siblings, or someone else who has regular contact with your parent and whose judgment you trust. This person may be able to help you figure out what it is that's bothering you, and then may be able to help you decide what you should do about it.

Another thing you can do is describe the situation to someone who's completely objective who may or may not know your parents. A friend or respected acquaintance may be able to give you some perspective on the situation.

Listen to the Concerns of Others

If others mention to you that they have noticed something worrisome about your parents, you should listen to what they have to say. Others may be more attuned to certain kinds of things than you are. You may not be aware that your dad isn't dressing with his usual attention to detail, but your sister, who's very appearance-conscious, might notice the change immediately.

Speak to Your Parent's Doctor

You may want to mention to your parent's physician that something strikes you as not quite right, or you may want to ask the doctor a question or two in order to clarify a concern that you might have. Some doctors will speak freely to the children of their patients, but because of the confidential nature of the doctor-patient relationship, it's best if you let your parent know that you plan to be talking with his doctor. Have him tell the doctor that you have permission.

Look for Repeated Patterns

If you don't feel comfortable putting in your two cents worth quite yet, you may want to wait and see if the problem develops into a more worrisome pattern. What you can do is continue to watch the situation and perhaps keep a written log of your observations. That way you'll know if the problem involves more than a few isolated incidents, and you'll have objective data to call upon if you need to make a case for your point of view.

If your dad smells of urine, you can make a note on your calendar every time you notice it. When you see that you were aware of it once in February, twice in March, and six times in April, you'll have a clearer picture of what you're dealing with.

Tell Your Parent Honestly but Tactfully About Your Concerns

When you know that you should say something to your father, it will help if you look for a comfortable, private opportunity to talk. Perhaps you could go for a ride in the car or for a walk together. You can begin the exchange by telling him in a calm and caring way that you're concerned about him. Try to avoid confronting him in such a way that he might interpret your message as a criticism. Instead of saying:

I don't care what you say, Dad. You've been limping for weeks. Something has got to be wrong with your leg. You need to have it looked at immediately.

You can say:

Dad, I'm really worried about you. I know you think that your limping isn't anything to get upset about. And I know that you don't like the idea of seeing the doctor. But I just want you to know that if you do want to go, I'd be happy to go with you if you'd like me to.

For most problems that your father may be having, you should try to discuss your concerns directly with him first. Then, if he isn't receptive, you can ask someone else in the family to mention the problem to him. Maybe your dad will get the message if he hears it from more than one person. However, for certain kinds of problems, it might be best to ask another person to intervene first. It probably would be less embarrassing for your dad if your mom told him that he should be changing his clothes more often because he smells bad.

As Doug drove his mother home, he asked her if she thought there was any chance that his father could in fact have a drinking problem. She looked over at him with an incredulous expression. She couldn't imagine how that could be possible because Charles was so capable in every way. He was very handy around the house, and he was totally in charge of all the banking and bill paying.

Still, Doug asked her if she minded if he poked around the place for a bit. She told him to go right ahead.

When they got to the house, the first place Doug headed for was his father's woodworking shop. After a quick look around, he found some gin bottles behind the paint cans and several empties in the trash.

He called his mother down. She was flabbergasted when she saw the bottles. Both of them were amazed at how Charles had been able to conceal this from them.

Doug called the doctor to tell her what he'd found. She told him that she appreciated the information. He said that he was embarrassed that he hadn't picked up on any of this earlier. She said that the families of people who abuse alcohol are often the last ones to realize what's going on.

Doug was worried about his dad, but he also felt a certain sense of relief. At least now he knew what the problem was.

Don't Put Yourself Down Because You Didn't Have a Crystal Ball

There may be times when you'll misjudge the situation and when you'll ignore problems that end up being serious. If this happens, try to remember that you're doing the best you can. Be easy on yourself. You're only human.

When Doug and his mother got to the hospital the next morning, they saw Charles' regular doctor. He told them that the head injury didn't look as though it would be a problem, but he said that Charles' disposition was another story. He'd been belligerent since early that morning, and they'd had to give him some medication to calm him down. The doctor also told them that the results of the laboratory tests were consistent with chronic alcohol abuse.

Doug and his mother listened somberly as the doctor went on to explain that he wanted to speak to Charles about his drinking and to try to get him into a recovery program. He invited them to come into the room with him, but he warned them that Charles was not in a good mood.

As the three of them walked down the hall, Doug wondered how his dad would respond. He was thankful that he and his mother had the doctor with them, and he hoped for the best.

Chapter 6

When Your Parents Won't Be Reasonable

Joe and his two brothers had no doubt that their ninety-four-year-old mother Louisa was an accident waiting to happen. It was a miracle that she was able to manage alone in her tiny apartment. Her eyesight and hearing were terrible, but she wore her glasses only when she could find them and used her hearing aid only when she felt like it. Her sense of balance wasn't very good, and she'd fallen quite a few times. Furthermore, she had long-standing diabetes and, as a result, the sensation in her hands and feet was not good and she'd sometimes burn or bruise herself without realizing it.

All three of Louisa's sons would have been more than happy to have their mother come and live with them. But she told them that she wouldn't want to live with any of their wives and besides, she liked having her own place where her great-grandchildren could come and have home-baked cookies (which children never got at home these days).

When they suggested that she move into a lovely retirement home, which they would be delighted to pay for, she told them that she'd never eat food that was prepared by strangers and that she hated being around old people.

And when they offered to hire someone to come in to do her housework, laundry, and shopping, she told them that she couldn't stand having anyone underfoot. She insisted that she was perfectly happy with things the way they were, "thank you very much."

Some parents accept their losses for what they are. They may struggle through an adjustment period when something goes wrong, but they're usually able to move ahead and make whatever adaptations are necessary. And other parents tend to exaggerate and overreact to their losses. They're often overanxious, and if they're allowed to, they'll happily become prematurely dependent on their adult children. And then there are others who won't face the fact that they can't do what they used to do. These are the people who won't make reasonable adjustments to their losses.

Those who won't be reasonable frequently manage to come up with some kind of convenient excuse that explains why they shouldn't have to make any changes in their lives.

If the issue is household help, they may refuse to hire someone because they don't want anyone to see their mess. Or they may not want to go through the inconvenience of the hiring process. Or they may be sure that they'll never find anyone who can do the job right. Or they may be convinced that it would be more trouble to supervise someone than to do the job themselves. Or they may not want to spend the money.

If the issue is moving to a smaller place, they may decide that it's not a good time to sell their house. Or they may not be able to bear to part with a single stick of furniture. Or they may not want to be too far away from their friends. Or they may be sure that they'll never find a place that will accept their pet. Or they may not be willing to give up the extra space that always comes in handy when the kids visit.

These kinds of people can be particularly exasperating to deal with, and if you have parents like these, you're faced with a special challenge. You can try to help them see what they're doing, but they may not listen to you. In fact, you may be the one person to whom they're least likely to listen, and they may take almost any suggestion you make as a personal criticism. When they reject your recommendations, your concern for them may become mixed with frustration and annoyance. You want to be respectful toward them, and you want to let them live their lives independently and with dignity, but you also want to look after their best interests and to protect them from harm.

One day Joe noticed that a burn on his mother's hand looked as if it had become infected. Despite her protests, he brought her to the doctor.

When Louisa was out of earshot, Joe mentioned to the doctor that he and his brothers had been trying to convince her to either move or get help. The doctor knew Louisa well enough to realize that they had their work cut out for them, so he suggested that they call the local geriatric assessment service. The staff there might be able to help them reason with her. Joe was grateful for the tip.

But the idea turned out to be a bust.

Joe spoke with a nurse at the assessment service, and she offered to speak with Louisa. But when he asked his mother if she'd talk with the nurse, she told him plainly that she wasn't the least bit interested and that she didn't understand why he was making such a big fuss.

Why Some Parents Are So Unreasonable

They're Having Trouble Accepting Their Losses

Some people don't seem to realize that they're no longer able to do many of the things that they could do when they were younger. They're unable to admit even to themselves that certain circumstances in their lives have changed irrevocably. And they may actually believe that they'll manage to do tomorrow what they haven't done in months or even years.

Your dad's car may have been sitting idle in the garage for as long as you can remember, but he may refuse to sell it or drop the insurance coverage on it because he could decide to renew his driver's license any day now. Your mom may be convinced that she'll clean all of the flammable material out of her attic just as soon as the weather cools off, even though she hasn't been up in the attic for years and even though she doesn't have enough energy to clean out her closet, much less her attic.

They're Desperately Holding on to Their Independence

Some people may be aware that they can't do what they used to do, but they are too inflexible to make any adjustments because of it. They've probably been independent all their lives, and they're undoubtedly quite proud of it. They know that they're having difficulties, but they prefer not to announce this unpleasant fact to the world. They don't want to take advice from their children, or from anyone else for that matter. And they'd rather struggle along than admit that they need help.

When you see your dad trying unsuccessfully to open a jar, you may offer to help him with it, but he may insist that he can do it himself. When you suggest to your mom that she should seriously consider moving to a building with an elevator, she may argue that she can manage the three flights of stairs in her building just fine.

If Nothing Else, They Have Their Pride

Some people are unwilling to admit to anyone that they're aging and that they need to make some adjustments because of it. They're terrified of anything that will make them look or feel old.

Your dad may think that hearing aids are fine for some folks but not for him. He may claim that he'd hear perfectly well if people would just stop mumbling so much. Your mom may prefer to sit at home all the time rather than go out with a cane because she doesn't want to look like a crippled old lady.

They Have a Thing About Money

Some people may acknowledge that they could use help, but they may refuse to pay for it or even let someone else pay for it. They may have been frugal all of their lives and may have always resisted spending money on anything that wasn't absolutely essential. They may be anxious that they won't have enough money left for the time when they really need it. They may find it inconceivable to pay someone else to help them do things that they think they should be able to do for themselves. They may be outraged by current prices compared to what they remember from years back. Or they may be determined to save their money so that they can leave something behind for their children.

They've probably worked hard, and most likely they've tried to save (and perhaps invest) their money so that they'd feel secure in their old age. But after years of preparing for the proverbial rainy day, they may not recognize that the day has finally arrived.

Handy Arrangements That Only Perpetuate the Problem

Sometimes when parents won't adjust to their losses, their children make matters worse by getting into Handy Arrangements with them. There are two characteristic ways that they do this. They either come to the rescue every time their parents need them, or they listen supportively every time their parents complain to them about their problems.

If you continually rescue your parents by doing things for them, they have no incentive to make any changes. Why should your mother accept a home-delivered meal service when you're willing to act as her short-order cook? Why should your father move to a more convenient location if you give him a ride every time he needs one?

And if you listen patiently to your parents' complaints and then offer suggestions to them, which they continually reject with one "yes, but" after another, you're also encouraging them to maintain the status quo. Your mother may grumble to you about how exhausted she is from taking care of your demented father, but she may refuse to hire the help that could make her life easier. If you listen to her, sympathize with her, and console her every time she complains, you're not helping her solve the problem. You're only helping to perpetuate it. The sympathy and attention that you give her may be so satisfying to her that she'd rather have them than get the help she needs.

Because Louisa wasn't cooperating, Joe and his brothers made an appointment to speak with the nurse at the geriatric assessment service themselves.

After hearing what their concerns were and asking a few pointed questions, the nurse explained to them that there was no way that they could prevent Louisa from staying in her own home or that they could force her to get help—unless they wanted to go to court and try to prove that she was incompetent. And based on what they'd told her, she seemed competent enough because she was, in fact, managing by herself. The nurse told them that even though it may make them nervous, Louisa had a right to live her life any way she wanted to. One day, something might happen that would make her see that she should move or get help. But in the meantime, all they could do was wait.

Joe and his brothers weren't thrilled to hear this, but they agreed to sit tight.

In order to stay as independent as possible, most elderly people set up routines that help them get through their days. If they stick to these routines, they can be reasonably sure that their shopping will get done, their meals will get cooked, and their bills will get paid. And because they've managed to get along pretty well so far, they strongly resist making any changes. They know instinctively that even a slight disruption in their lives could threaten their independence.

However, when your parents are taking risks that put their safety or health in jeopardy, you probably won't feel comfortable sitting idly by. You know that you should at least try to reason with them. But you also know better than to be so heavy-handed with your advice that they become resentful, dig their heels in further, and sabotage your efforts altogether.

The Bottom Line

Your folks will be more reasonable about making adjustments to their losses when they see for themselves that there's a genuine need for change.

How to Grease the Wheels of Change

Be Honest and Direct with Your Parents

If you're concerned about something, you should speak up and tell your parents what it is. Don't expect them to read your mind. For the moment, they may disregard what you're saying, but nonetheless, you're planting the seed of awareness in their consciousness. With time, they may come around. And besides, you'll feel better knowing that you've told them the truth as you see it.

Try to bring the problem to their attention in a nonconfrontational way. If you tell them how you feel instead of criticizing them, they'll be less inclined to argue with you. Instead of saying:

83

Dad, you've got to stop driving at night. What are you trying to prove at your age?

You can say:

 Dad, I get so upset whenever I hear that you've been driving at night. The thought of losing you in an accident really scares me.

Pick Your Battles Carefully

Try to concentrate on problems that are truly important. You don't have the time or energy to get worked up about every little thing that bothers you. This will only set up an adversarial relationship between you and your folks. If you nag them about the small stuff, they'll be less likely to listen to you when something that really matters comes up.

See If Another Family Member Can Reason with Your Parents

If the problem is serious enough and your folks aren't paying any attention to your concerns, you can ask a sibling or someone else in the family to speak with them. They might listen better to someone else than they will to you.

Help Your Parents See Their Options, and Then Back Off

Control is a prickly issue for many people, and your folks may be opposed to change because they sense that they're being manipulated or bossed around. You may be able to break through their resistance if you help them see that there are many options from which they can choose and that it's up to them to decide what they want to do. Then you can back off and let them make the next move.

This way they'll feel as though they still have some control. And the more control that they have over their own lives, the more agreeable they'll be.

Let the Situation Ripen

Even though you're worried about your folks, the situation can sometimes be safely left alone in the hope that reality will finally hit home.

You may invite your mother to spend a few weeks with you so that she can get her strength back after a bad bout of pneumonia. But she may insist on going directly back home after she's discharged from the hospital because she's sure that she'll do fine alone. What she may need to do is go home and struggle for awhile. Then she may realize how weak she really is, and then she may be willing to take you up on your offer after all.

This strategy may also be your best bet when your parents have a thing about money. As a general rule, you should encourage them to spend their money on things that will enhance their comfort and safety. But because deeply ingrained, fundamental attitudes about money won't change so easily, they may need to experience some discomfort or inconvenience before they finally admit to themselves that they have to dip into their savings or accept some financial help.

Try to Limit Your Involvement in Handy Arrangements

If you find that you're continually rescuing your parents or listening to their complaints, you may need to pull out of these Handy Arrangements before they'll be willing to change. When they're forced to struggle along without your help or support, the issue may be brought into better focus for them, and it may eventually dawn on them that they need to do things differently.

If you've been urging your mother to hire a book-keeper because you don't have the time to take care of her bills every month, you may need to simply stop helping her. Then, when the phone is disconnected because she hasn't paid the bill, she may concede that she needs to use a bookkeeping service. If you've been mowing your father's lawn for him because he won't hire a gardener, he may need to be at the receiving end of his neighbors' grumbling before he'll be willing to hire someone.

The same principle applies to your habit of listening to your parents when they complain. If your mom gripes all the time about how exhausted she is because of housework and if you continually sympathize with her, you may have to let her know that it's exasperating for you to hear this all the time. You may have to tell her that either she tries to get help or else she stops complaining because you don't want to hear about it any longer.

It won't be easy for you to pull out of these arrangements, and it won't be easy for you to stay out of them. It's hard to change the way you've been doing things once a pattern has been established. When you first tell your parents that the arrangement is going to have to stop, they probably won't be very happy about it. Moreover, as they try to adjust to the situation without your help or support, they may flounder around, take chances, and get themselves into trouble; this won't be a pleasant sight to see. In fact, you may worry about them so much that you end up reverting to your former arrangements.

Another possibility is that other people may fill in for you so that your parents will still have no reason to make any adjustments. You can try to explain to these well-meaning people that they're not doing anyone any favors, but ultimately you have no control over what they do.

Bring in an Outside Heavy

If your folks won't bend under sustained, cohesive family pressure, you can try to bring in a respected outsider who's not part of the family. Many unreasonable people will listen better to such a person than they will to their children. A good choice might be their doctor, another health professional with whom they've worked, their attorney, their clergyperson, or another authority figure who can be diplomatic but who has the clout to convince them that changes are in order.

You should make sure that the Outside Heavy hears the whole story ahead of time.

Take Drastic Action

In some situations, the stakes are so high that you can't fool around with hoping and praying. If you sincerely believe that your mother is truly no longer able to take care of her own physical needs, that she can't manage her financial affairs, or that she's vulnerable to being taken advantage of by others, you may have no other choice than to consult an attorney and go through the process of obtaining conservatorship over her.

In order to get conservatorship, you must demonstrate to a judge that your mother is incapacitated. If conservatorship is granted, a conservator (sometimes but not always a family member) is appointed by the court. This person would be empowered to make most decisions on your mother's behalf, even though they may be against her wishes.

Obtaining conservatorship can be quite expensive and time-consuming, and it involves a public proceeding. This is a choice which should be entered into only after careful consideration.

Get Help for Yourself If You Can't Let Go

Sometimes parents won't make reasonable adjustments to their losses despite all of the efforts of their children. If your parents aren't incapacitated, there are limits to what you can do. You have a right to speak your mind, but beyond that you may have to swallow hard and accept the fact that everyone is different and that you can't tell another person how to live. People can choose to ignore their medical problems, and they also can choose to take risks. There are just some things that you can't control.

You may have to face the criticism of others who don't understand why you're not forcing your parents to do what you think is right. And all you can do is tell these people that you've done everything you could. There's no reason to feel that you're being irresponsible.

If you're having a hard time living with the situation as it is, it's you who may be the one who needs to get help in order to learn how to let go. It may be a good idea for you to join a support group or get some counseling.

It wasn't easy, but Louisa's sons did their best to keep their mouths shut. Nothing too disastrous occurred for several months. But then, the inevitable happened.

Joe came by his mother's place one day to check on her and found her holding an icebag on her arm. Her wrist was swollen and tender. At first she played it down, but finally she admitted that she'd slipped while she was walking home from the market carrying two bags of groceries.

Joe sternly told Louisa that he was taking her to the emergency room. She winced in pain and didn't argue with him. It was a good thing she went because the doctor determined that she'd fractured her wrist and that she needed to have it repaired surgically.

Joe was furious. He'd told his mother many times that she should either call someone from the family or call a cab when she had a lot to carry home from the store. He couldn't take the worry anymore; he wasn't so young himself. She absolutely had to move or else get help.

When Your Folks Do Things That You Don't Like

Sometimes parents are adjusting pretty well to their losses, but they still do things that make their adult children angry. A recently-widowed father may marry a woman who's half his age, and his children may be convinced that she's only after his money. An elderly mother may give her piano to the housekeeper when her children have always had their eyes on it.

Again, you have to realize that there are limits to what you can do. You can't tell your parents how to run their lives. All you can do is share your feelings with them and hope that you can reason with them. Aside from that, you may have to learn to live with the situation—if you want to continue having a relationship with your parents. If you can't bear to watch what's going on, you may have to limit your contact with them. And if you can't distance yourself, you may want to get professional help.

Louisa got through the surgery fine. While she was recovering in the hospital, there were many heated negotiations between her and the three boys. She finally agreed to have a woman come in twice a week to do her cleaning, laundry, and shopping. Her sons weren't sure that this was going to be enough, but they figured that they'd better be happy with whatever concessions they could get out of their mother before she changed her mind. Within a few days, they came up with two good candidates, a very nice middle-aged lady and a student.

Louisa met both of them and chose the younger one.

But the setup didn't last long. Louisa couldn't stand having a stranger in her home, and as soon as her arm was out of the cast, the young woman was history.

▼

Chapter

7

When Your Siblings Aren't Doing Their Share

Annie was a hard-working supermom who led a busy, sometimes hectic, life. She was preparing a Moroccan feast for her part-time catering business when she got a call from her mother, Rose. Rose told her the bad news that Annie's father George had just flunked his driving test and that his license had been permanently revoked.

Rose and George were in their late seventies and lived in the same house they'd moved into when they were first married. Even though they'd slowed down in recent years, they were still in pretty good shape and loved working in their garden and taking part in local town meetings.

Rose was distraught. She'd never learned to drive, and she knew that she wasn't about to start now. Moreover, they lived far off the main road in a rural area that had no bus or taxi service. The last thing that she and George wanted to do was move, but they couldn't imagine how they'd get by without a car.

Annie didn't have an answer either, but she told her mother that she'd try to come up with something.

Unfortunately, the only thing she could think to do was to call her older brother Peter.

The Sometimes Shaky Sibling Alliance

As your folks get into their later years and begin to experience some of the losses of aging, you'll probably find yourself turning to your brothers and sisters for their support, advice, and assistance. This may be the first time since you were youngsters that you've had to interact closely with each other.

As you work together, it's possible that you and your siblings will agree on everything, that everyone will be supportive of one another, and that none of you will feel put upon. But it's also possible that things won't be quite so idyllic.

Highly-charged and long-buried unfinished business and juvenile rivalries may resurface and cause friction between you. And there may be unspoken concerns about what's happening with your parents' money or about who's going to inherit what when they pass on.

It's also possible that you and your siblings may have differences of opinion about how to go about doing things. One of you may insist that your parents desperately need housekeeping help, whereas the other may be convinced that a little dust is nothing to get worked up about. One of you may prefer to look for an inexpensive cleaning person, while the other may think it would be much better to hire a more expensive bonded professional from an agency.

And finally, your parents themselves may cause discord between you and your brothers and sisters. They may make promises, do favors, or give gifts that drive wedges between you. They may help one child out financially when the others don't think that this person deserves any help at all. They may spend more time with one set of grandchildren than with another. They may criticize the adult child who's helping them out while they put the one who's doing nothing for them on an undeserved pedestal.

Annie's brother Peter was a hot-shot architect whose life was even more hectic than Annie's. His wife was in real estate, and they had a live-in nanny to care for their young son. Peter lived only an hour away from his folks, but he'd never been particularly attentive to them. It was Annie who kept in close touch with them and helped them when they needed something.

Annie reached Peter on his car phone and told him about their parents' problem. He wasn't happy to hear that his dad had lost his license, but he didn't think it was the end of the world. He figured that Annie could help them with any driving they needed or that she could arrange for someone else to do it. If that didn't work out, their folks would just have to sell their house and move closer to town.

Annie tried to explain to him how badly Rose and George wanted to stay in their home, and she tried to make it clear to him that if they were going to stay, they'd need some help. She told him that the responsibility was too much for her to handle alone.

But Peter didn't get it. In fact, he was annoyed that she was even bothering him. He told her that he was under tremendous pressure at work and that he'd try to call their parents more often, but that was all he could do.

Annie was disgusted with her brother for being unwilling to pitch in, but she wasn't surprised by his lack of consideration, so she didn't bother to argue with him.

The Loneliness of the Primary Caregiver

In many families, one child ends up providing the bulk of the care for the aging parents and the other children assume a more secondary role or no role at all. The Primary Caregiver may be the child who lives nearest the folks, the one who has the closest relationship with them, or the one who's simply the most able and willing to do the job. More often than not, this person is a daughter. And if a daughter isn't available, sometimes a daughter-in-law will step forward.

Of course, adult children who have no siblings automatically become sole caregivers for their parents, and this has its advantages as well as its disadvantages. On the one hand, they don't have to consider the opinions of anyone else, and there's no one for them to resent for not being sufficiently helpful. On the other hand, they have to make all the decisions and shoulder the burden entirely alone, and there's no one with whom they can share their complaints and worries.

If you do have siblings, and if you're the Primary Caregiver for your parents, you probably can look back and see how you unwittingly slipped into the role. Most likely, in the beginning you didn't give much thought to the little things you did to help them out. Perhaps you did a few of the heavy chores around their place, installed some safety equipment for them, connected them up with some resources for seniors in their community, or stayed with one of them while the other was in the hospital. None of this was particularly demanding, and you did what needed to be done without thinking that much about it. And in many ways it was probably simpler for you to do it all yourself. That way you didn't have to check with your brothers and sisters or worry about their opinions or their schedules. You could call all the shots.

Annie took it upon herself to do what she could for her folks. She advertised for local teens to do some driving for them, she asked their friends and neighbors if they'd be willing to help out occasionally, and she found out about a senior citizens' van service that could take them into town once a week for a small fee.

For their part, Rose and George did their best to get along without a car. They were good about using the van, although it embarrassed George to be driven around with a "bunch of old ladies." And their friends helped out when they could. But the hired drivers never lasted very long, nor were they particularly reliable.

Annie called her parents every morning to make sure that they had everything they needed for the day, and she took the half-hour trip out to their place a few times a week to help them with errands. This wasn't a terrible hardship for her, but it was a significant addition to her already packed schedule.

When she mentioned to her folks that Peter should be doing more to help them out, they insisted that they didn't want to put any demands on him because his career was so time-consuming. And because Annie knew how proud they were of him, she let it go. But she wasn't happy with the situation.

Then, a few weeks later she dropped off some groceries at her parents' house and discovered that George was laid up in bed. Apparently, he'd climbed up on a ladder to put the storm windows on and had fallen and strained his back.

She demanded to know why he hadn't asked his perfectly able-bodied son to do the job.

He told her that he hadn't wanted to bother Peter and that his injury wasn't anything serious.

But it was serious enough for Annie. As far as she was concerned, she and her brother had to talk.

The Moment of Reckoning

When you're the Primary Caregiver for your folks and they're experiencing only minor problems, you may think that you can take care of everything yourself. But sooner or later as more serious difficulties develop, you may discover that you've taken on more than you can handle. You may finally realize that you can't continue to do it all alone and that it's time for your brothers and sisters to step in and do their part.

But by this time you're stuck in a pattern that's very hard to change, and your siblings may not be particularly willing to cooperate. They may feel put out when you tell them that you can't do everything yourself, and they may come up with any number of excuses that explain (in their minds at least) why they're not able to do more than they're already doing. They thought you were handling things so well. What happened all of a sudden?

The Bottom Line

If you want your siblings to do their share, you've got to get them actively involved in your folks' lives from early on.

How to Get Your Siblings Involved

Keep Them Up on Things

It is important that you keep your brothers and sisters fully informed about anything significant that's going on in your parents' lives and that you keep them abreast of things as they happen. You should, for example, let them know when your folks have a health problem, when they're going on a trip, and when they're planning to make a major purchase. At times this may seem unnecessary and cumbersome because your siblings may not need to do anything about the situation. Nevertheless, they'll feel much more connected with your parents if they know what's going on.

Listen to What They Have to Say

If you want your siblings to do their share, you'll have to consider their suggestions and find ways to make compromises with them when you have differences of opinion. You may have trouble doing these things if you're the kind of person who likes to be in control. When your siblings offer their ideas, you may tend to disregard them. And when they do help you out, you may criticize their efforts. Then, when they pull back and stop helping, you may accuse them of leaving you with the whole responsibility. Whatever they do, they can't win. Unless you want to be the sole caregiver for your parents (and unless you promise not to complain about it), you're going to have to relinquish some control. You can't have it both ways.

Make Sure Your Parents Understand That You Need Your Siblings' Help

Explain to your parents that you can't do everything yourself and that you expect your brothers and sisters to help out. Assure them that everyone who wants to can find some way to help. If your parents think that your siblings should be excused from taking on any responsibilities, try to take a constructive approach rather than an argumentative one. Instead of saying:

Listen, Mom. I really don't care all that much about Phyllis' health. What about mine? If she doesn't start pulling her weight, I'm the one who's going to get sick.

You can say:

I can see how worried you are about Phyllis' health, Mom. And I know that she may never be able to do as much as I'm doing, but I think it's only right that she does something. Maybe she can be the one to check in with you every day on the phone.

If You Want Your Siblings' Help, Tell Them So

You can't expect your brothers and sisters to guess what your needs are. You have to let them know that you could use some help. But try to tell them in a nonconfrontational way. Instead of ordering them around, you can ask them what they'd like to do. If they can't come up with any ideas, offer them a few possibilities, and give them the opportunity to choose something themselves. If they decide on their own what they're going to do, they'll be more likely to do it. Instead of saying:

You water the plants and pick up the mail while Dad's in the hospital. I'll pay the bills.

You can say:

When Dad's in the hospital, the plants have to be watered, the mail has to be picked up, and the bills have to be paid. What would fit best into your schedule?

Remember That Even Siblings Who Live Far Away Can Help

Even if your brothers and sisters live a good distance from you and your parents, they still can help your parents out. They can call and write them regularly. They can invite them to their homes for visits. They can come to stay with them once in a while so that you can get away. They can contribute money so you can hire someone to help you out. They can check with you regularly to see if you need anything. And at the very least, they can let you know that they care and that they appreciate what you're doing. Emotional support can be extremely important, and it can help you keep up the energy and the will to continue on. It's something that anyone can give regardless of distance, family circumstances, or financial limitations.

Be Sure to Give Your Siblings Positive Feedback

Everyone enjoys a well-deserved pat on the back. When your brothers and sisters feel that their efforts are appreciated, they'll be more likely to stay involved. So let them know how much you value their help.

Speak Up Right Away When There's a Problem Between You and Your Siblings

If you're having a disagreement with your brothers and sisters, if you feel that you're not getting the cooperation you need from them, or if you don't like the way they're doing things, the best thing to do is to speak up as soon as there's any hint of trouble. Don't wait until you're so fed up that you can't be calm and rational. Instead of saying:

I've been filling Daddy's insulin syringes myself for months now and you haven't offered to help one damn time.

You can say:

Now that Daddy's on insulin, he'll need to have syringes filled every week. Let's get together and figure out some way we can share the responsibility.

After you've talked with them about the problem, you may achieve a better sense of mutual understanding—even though you may not resolve the problem exactly the way you wanted to. In some cases, a family meeting with the folks may be in order. And in especially sticky situations, you might want to consult a counselor or a mediator.

Divide Up the Duties

Because everyone has a different style of doing things, it may help if you and your siblings have separate areas of responsibility that don't overlap too much. If your sister often forgets to pick up your father's medicine when it's her week to do so, and you frequently have to remind her, perhaps the two of you shouldn't be sharing the chore. You can be in charge of the medicine, and your sister can do something entirely different.

Consider Bringing Highly-charged, Unspoken Issues Out in the Open

If concerns about money or the inheritance are complicating your relationship with your siblings, you can try to bring the subject up with them, and they may welcome the opportunity to talk about it. In addition, you may want to consider arranging a family meeting so that all of you can hear together what your folks' wishes are. Perhaps then any misunderstandings can be cleared up.

But keep in mind that you may be stirring things up more than you intended to when you bring up these kinds of issues. Money can be symbolic of love, power, and control; you'll have to use your own judgment and decide if a frank discussion would be worth it or not.

Instead of Making Accusations, Share Your Feelings

When you criticize your siblings, you put them on the defensive and often end up starting an argument. So instead of putting them on the spot, try to tell them how you feel. If you do this, they may respond more positively to your concerns. Instead of saying:

 You never do anything to help.

You can say:

 It's very hard for me to take care of everything myself.

Help Them Find Solutions to Their Stumbling Blocks

Even with all your efforts, your brothers and sisters may still not become as involved with your folks as you'd like them to be, and they may come up with any number of reasons for this. They don't have enough time. The folks like you better. Their spouses are preventing them from doing more. They can't stand nursing homes. It's too painful for them to see the folks in their declining years.

Instead of challenging the excuses that they give, try to discuss the situation with them, and try to pinpoint exactly where the stumbling blocks lie. Then see if you can work together to find a creative way to solve the problem.

If your brother can't stand nursing homes, ask him what it is about them that he hates. If he finds it depressing to see the other debilitated patients, or if the smell makes him sick to his stomach, he may be able to arrange for an aide to bring your father out on the patio for their visits. If he feels queasy every time he sees your father's catheter bag, perhaps he'd be willing to visit if the nurse moved it to the other side of the bed where it would be out of his sight.

Try to Help Them Get to the Bottom of the Real Problem

When you can't find a way to get around the stumbling block, or when your brothers and sisters say that they'll help but then renege on their promises, it's a pretty sure bet that there's something else going on beneath the surface. It may be that they have a bad relationship with the folks. They may be angry at them because of past injustices, either real or imagined. They may see negative qualities in them that they also see in themselves. Or perhaps they may find that being around them brings out feelings of helplessness and fear in the face of aging and death.

If your brothers and sisters are willing to talk with you about these things, take the time to explore them together. But keep in mind that solving the problem won't be easy. They may not have enough insight to identify the underlying issues. They may not be willing to be honest with you about their feelings. And even if they can and will do these things, the issues may be so old, so deep, and so complex that a few conversations won't be enough to unravel it all. But at least your conversations may bring about more mutual understanding and respect. (And perhaps they'll become motivated to get some professional counseling.)

Don't Be Surprised if the Arrangement Isn't Perfectly Fair

One sibling may have more time, more energy, more money, or fewer obligations than another; so allowances may have to be made for these kinds of individual differences. An absolutely fair and equitable distribution of responsibilities may be almost impossible to achieve. You'll have to decide how hard to push your siblings if they're not as involved as you'd like them to be.

If you're spending more time caring for the folks than they are, perhaps your family can agree to compensate you in some way.

If the Situation Is Hopeless, Reconcile Yourself to the Idea of Going It Alone

As you make the effort to work out problems that come up between you and your siblings, remember that deeply ingrained habits and long-established patterns of behavior are extremely difficult to change. You may find that dealing with a particular brother or sister creates so many insurmountable problems that it's not worth the effort. If he or she is totally unreliable, has serious emotional or substance abuse problems, is verbally or physically abusive, or, for any other reason, is hindering you more than helping you, perhaps you should stop setting yourself up for disappointment. You may be better off going it alone.

If you've decided to be the sole caregiver for your parents (or if you're an only child), it's important that you try to find some kind of support system. Your parents' own siblings as well as other relatives, their friends and neighbors, and perhaps even individuals such as a mail carrier, a gardener, or a barber would be willing to get involved in some capacity. These people may never feel the same sense of responsibility toward your parents that you do, but they can make the burden easier on you if you let them help.

Annie called Peter and insisted that they meet for lunch as soon as possible. She told him that she needed to talk about George's accident. After a little prodding, he managed to fit her in.

A few days later at lunch, Annie made it clear that she'd reached her limit. She told Peter in no uncertain terms that Rose and George were his folks too, and that she expected him to become involved. He wasn't the only one with demands on his time.

Peter was surprised by the intensity of her anger. He offered to give her money so that she could hire someone to help her out.

Annie forced herself to remain calm and told him that this wasn't about money and it wasn't about hiring help. She took a deep breath and admitted that the situation was partly her fault. She'd thought she could do it all herself, but she'd been wrong. She needed his support. Their folks could rely on others to some extent, but ultimately their kids were the ones who'd make it possible for them to stay in their home.

For once, Peter didn't have a glib response, and Annie could see that she was finally getting through to him. She told him that she'd given it a lot of thought and that she'd be willing to call their parents regularly and go by their place once a week to help them out—but once a week only. They discussed a number of possible arrangements, and Peter finally agreed to spend one weekend morning a month with Rose and George. He'd help them with chores around the house and do any driving that was needed. Plus, he'd be in phone contact with them on the weekends.

Annie and Peter both felt that they'd come to about as fair an agreement as they could reasonably expect. When they said goodbye, they gave each other an awkward but heartfelt hug.

Caring for your aging parents can be a lengthy and difficult commitment. Whatever you and your brothers and sisters can do to come to an accommodation will be well worth the effort, and you'll discover that there are many benefits to working together. Despite the inevitable ups and downs, you'll find that as you share the responsibilities, you'll grow closer, you'll achieve a new level of intimacy and honesty, and you'll gain a better appreciation of each other.

It was a year later, and Annie's arrangement with Peter worked out even better than she'd expected. She felt much more relaxed now that she could count on him and share her concerns with him, and Rose and George were able to stay in their home.

But the thing that no one had predicted was Peter's mid-life crisis. It turned out that he'd been having an affair with a young architect in his firm. One day he announced that he was leaving his wife and that he and his girlfriend were planning to move to the other coast.

It looked like Annie was on her own again.

Chapter 8

When Your Parents Live Far Away

Helen was an active retired journalist who liked to get things done. She'd never had much patience with her timid little mother, Pearl. Pearl lived more than halfway across the country from her, and her two brothers lived even farther away from their mother. Helen visited with Pearl at least once a year, and they talked on the phone to each other every Sunday.

On several occasions, Helen had suggested to her mother that she give up her apartment and move into a senior retirement community close to her, but Pearl wasn't interested. She had friends where she was, and she was active in her church. Helen was concerned that there weren't any family members close by to keep an eye on her mother, but so far, Pearl's only significant problem had been a high blood pressure condition for which she took medication.

During Helen's most recent visit, however, she noticed that her mother's ankles were swollen. She asked her how long this had been going on, and Pearl said that it had been a few months. Helen was annoyed that her mother hadn't said anything to her about it. But Pearl explained that she'd been keeping her feet *elevated, and that this had helped. And besides, she hadn't wanted to worry her.*

When your parents live far away, the problems that come up are not all that different from the ones that arise when your folks live down the street. But the challenges of long-distance caregiving certainly can feel more daunting.

Because you're not there with your folks all the time, you can't always see for yourself what's going on, and even if you visit them often, you may never feel as though you have a complete picture of the situation. Your parents may not be telling you the whole story, or they may be telling you a slightly distorted version of the truth because they don't want to worry you, bother you, or admit that something is wrong. Or they may have been exaggerating their problems so much that you've stopped taking what they say seriously.

Furthermore, you may feel anxious because you're not at all familiar with the resources in your parents' area and you don't have the slightest idea how to go about figuring them out.

Helen was concerned about her mother's swollen ankles, but she knew that Pearl would do anything to avoid seeing a doctor. She told her that she wanted to make an appointment for her. Pearl could sense her daughter's irritation, so she didn't argue.

At the appointment, the doctor questioned Pearl carefully and examined her. He discovered that she had a mild case of congestive heart failure. She hadn't been in to see him in years, and the blood pressure medication that she'd been taking wasn't doing its job anymore. He took her off of it and put her on water pills and liquid potassium for this more serious condition.

Helen was worried. Congestive heart failure didn't sound like something to be taken lightly. She was angry at herself for not insisting that Pearl see her doctor regularly.

When Helen got ready to go back home, she instructed her mother to let both the doctor and her know right away if she developed any problems at all.

Because your parents live far away from you, you may feel guilty that you're not there to do more for them. And then, when you do go to visit them and you do spend time helping them out with something, your family back home may resent the fact that you're not there with them. This of course only makes you feel even more guilty.

And then you may be angry with your siblings because they aren't doing more to help you out.

Helen called her mother every few days to make sure that she was all right. But a week after she'd gotten home, Helen got a call in the middle of the night from Pearl's neighbor. The woman told her that she was at the hospital with her mother. Pearl had apparently left the water running in the tub. The tub had overflowed and water had leaked into the apartment below. The tenant in that apartment had awakened the building supervisor. He'd banged on Pearl's door but got no response, so he let himself into her apartment to turn the water off. He found Pearl sitting in her living room looking befuddled and making absolutely no sense whatsoever. He didn't know what to do with her, so he brought her to their apartment, and they'd taken her to the hospital.

Helen's mind was racing. She thanked the woman profusely for all her help and told her that she'd call the hospital and would take care of things from there on in. They could go on home.

As soon as she hung up, Helen called the emergency room, but the nurse told her to call back in an hour when they'd know more. So Helen paced around her bedroom for an hour and then called back. This time the nurse had some news. The doctor had found that Pearl's blood chemistry was out of balance. They'd put her on an intravenous solution, and she was resting comfortably. They'd know more in the next day or so.

Helen was scared, and she felt a headache coming on.

When some kind of crisis comes up, there may be occasions when you'll have to use your vacation time or take a leave of absence from work in order to be with your parents. And if the situation gets worse or if the crises become more frequent, you may end up spending a great deal of money on phone calls and plane flights. These added complications can only make you feel even more anxious and resentful.

There was no question in Helen's mind that she had to go back to be with her mother, so she made several calls and was finally able to book an early morning flight. Then she threw some clothes in her suitcase and made a long list of things for her husband to take care of while she was gone.

The next morning, after virtually no sleep, she kissed her not-particularly-happy husband good-bye and headed to the airport. When she got there, she called both of her brothers to let them know what was going on. They were glad that she was on top of things and asked her to keep them posted.

She arrived in her mother's city late that afternoon and grabbed a cab to the hospital. Her mother was sleeping, and the nurse told her that Pearl was doing better and that the doctor planned to discharge her in the next day or two. According to the nurse, her mother had stopped taking her potassium because she didn't like its bitter taste, and the resulting potassium imbalance had caused her to become temporarily delirious.

There's no question that long-distance caregiving can be a difficult challenge. There are, however, some ways that you can minimize the hassles.

The Bottom Line

When you live far away from your parents and you're worried about them, you'll make things much easier on yourself if you set up a Long-Distance Safety Net.

How to Set Up a Long-Distance Safety Net

Try to Maintain an Honest and Open Relationship with Your Parents

When your parents live far away, it's especially important that you do your best to communicate well with them and that you go to the trouble to understand things from their perspective. You don't have the luxury of time to make your own assumptions about what they really mean when they're trying to tell you something. And similarly, there's no time to give them subtle hints about what you'd like them to do and then cross your fingers and hope that they understood what you meant.

If something concerns you, your best bet is to tell them exactly what it is. If the communication between you is good, they'll be more inclined to listen to what you have to say, and they'll be more likely to let you know when something is going wrong at their end.

Don't Do Things for Your Parents Behind Their Backs

Any changes that you help your parents make should be carried out with their full knowledge and consent. If you know that you have their complete agreement, you can go back home and be fairly certain that things will proceed as planned. It's not worth it to try to put something over on them.

If you hire a gardener when they don't think they need one, they're likely to fire him the minute you leave town. Then you'll be back to square one, and you'll have to negotiate an arrangement with them all over again. When there are many miles between you, this can get expensive and time-consuming, not to mention aggravating.

Make Extra Sure That Your Siblings Do Their Share

If your siblings aren't pitching in enough, you can try to suggest some concrete things that they can do to help, and it's a good idea for you to get in the habit of speaking to them about your folks on a regular basis. If you compare notes with them and listen with an open mind to their suggestions, there's a greater likelihood that they'll help you out and back you up when you need their support.

Make the Best Possible Use of Your Time When You Visit Your Parents

When you visit your parents, you should make it your business to talk frankly with them about how they're managing and to suggest necessary modifications and adjustments. It's especially important that they take all appropriate safety precautions and that they're taking full advantage of any convenience measures and special equipment that will enable them to stay more independent than they would be otherwise.

If you're planning a brief visit to help them in their dealings with agencies, be sure to set up your appointments ahead of time. Many agency people have busy schedules and may not be able to see you on the spur of the moment.

Become Acquainted with the Other Important People in Your Parents' Lives

With your parents' knowledge, you should make it a point to introduce yourself to as many of the key people in their lives as you can.

It's a good idea to stop by and speak to their friends and neighbors. They're the ones who see your parents often and who might pick up on any problems that they're having. If any of them offer to help you and if you think they're sincere about it, find out what it is that they'd like to do and then take them up on it. People feel useful and needed if they can do things for others in some small way, so you shouldn't think that you're imposing on them. From time to time, you can tell them how much you appreciate their efforts, and you also can send them an occasional note or gift.

In addition, you might want to think about speaking to some other people with whom your parents have regular contact. This list could include their physician, their attorney, their banker, and their clergyperson. And if it's possible, you can try to meet with these folks face-to-face so that the connection between you will be more personal.

Many of these people will know how your parents are functioning better than you will, and they may be able to catch problems before the difficulties get out of hand. If your mother's banker notices that she keeps coming into the bank with questions and that she never seems to get things right, he can let you know. You may decide to hire a bookkeeper to help her with her financial affairs, and this decision could prevent her from making an embarrassing and possibly expensive mistake.

Let all of these people know about any special concerns that you have. Then make sure that they have your telephone number, and encourage them to call you collect if they have any important information to share with you about your parents. And you can give them a call if you feel uneasy about something.

Find a Pro Who Knows the Ropes in Your Parents' Area

If your parents need to make a change in their lives, an expert who works in their community can be extremely valuable. He or she can get you hooked up with the right resources, can save you much time, and can help you avoid many hassles.

You can start by calling your parents' local Area Agency on Aging to get some ideas about where to begin. The people there will usually be able to point you in the right direction.

If It Becomes Necessary, Hire Someone to be Your Surrogate

If the urgent calls from your parents become too frequent, it may be worth it for you to hire another person to do some of the things that you'd do for them if you lived closer. This person could stop by regularly to check on them and could help them with any little problems that come up. You could hire almost any responsible person for this job.

However, if your parents' situation is particularly complicated or if they're difficult to work with, you might want to consider retaining a private geriatric care manager. He or she may be able to save you a great deal of worry as well as time and money by maintaining regular and direct contact with your parents, by keeping you posted on what's happening with them, by helping them solve any problems that come up, and by taking care of hiring the help that they need. Also, many care managers have counseling skills, so they might be effective in convincing your parents to hire help when they aren't so sure that they need it.

Consider Moving Your Parents Closer to You

The decision to uproot your parents from the community in which they live should never be taken lightly. Unless they've been to your area to visit often, unless their visits have been extended ones over the years, and unless they've developed a social network of their own in your area, the transition to the new community could create a whole new set of difficulties for them. It may be more convenient for you to have them near you, and there may come the time when such a move is necessary. But you should know that

111

they could end up being dependent on you. It's not easy for older people to get out and make new friends, so they may look to you as a replacement for all of the people who used to give their world a sense of comfort and stability.

If your parents are thinking about moving closer to you, it might be a good idea for them to come for a long visit before they sell their home or give up their apartment. This way they'll see exactly what they're getting into. And before they do anything, they should give a lot of thought to what they'll be losing.

There will be times when moving closer to you can be a good solution. It may be the right choice if they want to make the move very much, if they no longer have many close friends or family members in their area, and if they must move to some sort of care facility and have no one else to look in on them.

When Pearl woke up, she was very happy to see her daughter, but Helen didn't waste any time and demanded to know why in the world her mother had stopped taking her medicine. Pearl was very embarrassed. She told Helen that the potassium had tasted vile and that she hadn't realized how important it was to take it. She promised her that it wouldn't happen again and asked her to please explain everything to the neighbors. Helen assured her that she would.

When Pearl was discharged from the hospital, her doctor arranged for a nurse from a home health agency to go by her place to make sure that she was taking her medicine properly and to check her blood levels. Helen spent the next few days with her mother until she was satisfied that she was going to be all right.

Before she left however, Helen wanted to make sure that Pearl would be watched after better than she had been before. So she arranged to call the home health agency nurse a few times a week to check on how things were going. She also met with a few of her mother's friends and neighbors and asked them to call her collect if they noticed anything at all unusual about Pearl. And finally, she spoke with her brothers who agreed to step up their calls and visits.

Get Support for Yourself If You Need It

Being a long-distance caregiver can be a strain, especially if you're trying to juggle the responsibility while you also have heavy-duty family and work demands. If the stress is getting to you, it might be useful for you to join a support group and meet other adult children who are struggling with similar issues. It can help to know that you're not alone.

When Helen headed back home, she felt a little more at ease now that she had a safety net in place, but she wasn't totally relaxed about the situation by any means. She thought again about asking her mother to move closer to her, but she wasn't at all sure that it was such a great idea.

When You're Worried About Your Parents' Mental Health

One day Jan got a call from her widowed mother, Roslyn. Roslyn had just received a letter informing her that in three months she was going to be evicted from her apartment because her building was being torn down to make way for a minimall. Her mother couldn't believe it. This had been her home for 40 years, and it was packed with mementos of her life. She was appalled that the law would allow elderly tenants to be thrown out into the street just like that.

As soon as Jan heard this upsetting news, she began to feel anxious because her mother had never been one to react well to change. Jan tried to be supportive and upbeat and assured Roslyn that there were plenty of nice apartments available. She told her that she'd help her find one and that she'd assist her with the move. For the time being, she asked her mother to look through the listings in the paper and circle any places that seemed promising.

In a few weeks, she'd come into town and take her around to look at them.

But her mother's response wasn't encouraging. She was convinced that she'd never find anything decent at an affordable price.

That evening, Jan called her sister who lived across the country to tell her what had happened. Both of them knew that the next few months were not going to be easy.

When Older People Are Troubled and Unhappy

As people move into old age, they usually bring along with them whatever emotional problems they've had in the past. Then they're forced to deal with the losses of aging and the stresses that go along with being an elderly person in our culture. People who have done well throughout their lives often continue to do well despite these additional problems. But those who've had their share of difficulties in the past often have an even harder time of it when they get older.

In our society, emotional problems are often ignored, misunderstood, or covered up. And even when such problems develop into full-blown psychiatric illnesses, they're still often regarded as less important than physical illnesses. This sentiment is reflected in the fact that many insurance companies provide much more limited coverage for emotional problems than they do for physical ones.

Because of these attitudes, adult children often try to push their parents' troubles out of their minds. They may figure that their parents have good reason to be unhappy. They may think that what they're seeing is only a temporary exaggeration of their parents' usual way of behaving. They may assume that their parents' behavior probably is normal for older people. They may be convinced that there's not much that can be done because of their parents' age. They may believe that it's not worth it to put their elderly parents through the rigors of treatment. They may be embarrassed because they think that their parents' difficulties reflect poorly on themselves and their families. They may assume that their parents would refuse to get help for problems of this kind. And they may not feel comfortable talking about these kinds of things with their folks.

Physicians share many of these same misconceptions, and they too don't always recognize mental health problems for what they are. Furthermore, when they do acknowledge that their elderly patients have emotional difficulties, they often feel ill-equipped to do anything about them.

A week and a half later, Jan arrived to take her mother apartment hunting and discovered that Roslyn hadn't even looked at the listings. Jan was annoyed and asked her what was going on. Roslyn's only response was that nothing would be worth looking at. Jan tried to contain her anger. Then she sat down and went through the paper herself. When she was finished, she told her mother to put on her coat.

The two of them spent the next few hours looking at several perfectly nice apartments, but Roslyn took no interest in any of them. By the end of the afternoon, Jan was feeling aggravated, but she decided not to push things. They had a few months to find a place. She'd wait until her mother got used to the idea of moving before she took her out looking again.

When she got home, Jan called her sister to vent her frustration. Her sister agreed that their mother was being a real pain.

Some of the Mental Health Problems That Burden Older People

Depression

Depression is by far the most common emotional problem in the general population, and it's especially prevalent among the elderly. When depression in an older person isn't properly diagnosed and treated, it can lead to unnecessary retirement, the overuse of social and medical services, needless hospitalizations and nursing home admissions, and the alienation of families and friends.

Everybody feels down and blue from time to time, but because of the many losses that older people go through, they probably experience this feeling more often than younger people do. In addition, older folks sometimes have trouble coping with stress because they don't have the physical and emotional reserves that younger people have.

After a significant loss, most people go through a natural, necessary, and appropriate grieving period; and in most cases they recover from their grief with time and with support from others. But sometimes the sadness doesn't lift and people become so overcome with anxiety, fear, and anger that they become drained and inert. When this happens, they can become so depressed that they're no longer able to relate to the world around them or function on a daily basis.

People with major depression find no joy in activities that once gave them pleasure. They lose their appetites. They have difficulty sleeping. They have very little energy. They have problems concentrating. They feel as though they're worthless. And they sometimes can become suicidal.

Antidepressant medication has proved itself to be effective in treating depression. With these drugs, depressed people often find that their moods are elevated from depressed to normal. Then when they start to feel better, they often sleep better and eat better, and they're sometimes willing to get into therapy or into other activities that can help them get out of their depression.

Sometimes, counseling alone is sufficient in treating cases of mild or moderate depression. But many older people are unwilling to have anything to do with psychotherapy because they don't see it as having any value or because they think that it's only for those who are crazy or weak.

In extreme cases of depression, other treatment approaches are sometimes necessary. When people haven't responded to medication, when they can't tolerate its side effects, or when they're suicidal, electroconvulsive therapy can be very effective. And psychiatric hospitalization is sometimes valuable as well.

Anxiety

Anxiety is fairly common among elderly people who often have plenty to worry about and have little else to occupy their time and attention. These folks often feel better if they get involved in some kind of activity, get into counseling, get more exercise, or take steps to reduce stress in their lives. They also can be helped if they use relaxation techniques, such as meditation, hypnosis, and biofeedback. But these techniques will help only if they believe that such approaches can work for them and if they're willing to practice them regularly.

Sometimes when people act as though they're anxious and restless, they're actually suffering from depression. If they respond to antidepressant drugs, there's a good chance that depression is their real problem.

Other people suffer from what are known as anxiety disorders. These are characterized by terrifying feelings of panic (panic attacks), unreasonable fears of specific objects or situations (phobias), or obsessive thoughts and senseless compulsive acts (obsessive-compulsive disorders). Those who suffer from anxiety disorders usually know that what they're experiencing isn't normal, and their behavior causes them great distress.

Minor tranquilizers can be useful as a temporary treatment for disabling anxiety. But the trouble with these drugs is that they can be highly addictive, and people often find that they must take them in increasingly larger doses in order to get good results. Tranquilizers also have a sedating effect and can cause some individuals to become depressed, to lose their concentration, and to get confused.

For these reasons, the best way for people to deal with extreme anxiety is to combine tranquilizers with psychotherapy. Therapy can enable them to get to the root of their problems or to deal with their feelings in healthier ways so that they eventually can get off the medication.

Paranoia

When elderly people begin to act paranoid, there are a few possible explanations for their behavior that should be ruled out.

The first thing that should be done is to have their hearing and vision evaluated because their disturbed thinking could be based on misinformation. If your mother hears poorly, she may suspect that others are whispering about her.

Another thing to check out is whether what they're claiming to be true is actually the case. Con artists know that others tend to discount what older people say. It's possible that your mother's cleaning lady is in fact taking her jewelry.

Additionally, it's a good idea to find out if they have a poor understanding of what's going on because others aren't taking the time to explain things to them. Your mom's bank may be going out of business, but if she doesn't know this, she could think that she's the only person in the world who must move her account.

And finally, they should see a physician so that dementia can be ruled out. If your mother is experiencing memory loss, she may be certain that her neighbor has stolen her hairbrush because she can't find it anywhere.

Once other explanations have been eliminated, you may have to consider the possibility that your parent is truly paranoid. True paranoia is referred to as delusional disorder. Those who suffer from this relatively rare condition are preoccupied with the fixed and false belief that some person or thing is out to harm them or has some special power. Their delusions begin with something small that's based on a kernel of truth and develop over time into elaborate systems. Most of the time, paranoid people are able to function well on a daily basis and think in a clear and orderly way, but their delusions usually disrupt their social relationships and frighten others off.

People with a delusional disorder rarely seek help because they don't believe that they have a problem. They come to public attention when they instigate a lawsuit based on their delusions or when they harass the police or social service agencies in seeking help to combat their persecutors. At this point, their families often are forced to get them into treatment.

Antipsychotic drugs can be effective in treating paranoia; but as soon as people start to think more normally, they often deny the value of the medication and stop taking it. Then the cycle begins all over again. But if they're willing to get into psychotherapy while they're taking the drugs, they sometimes can be convinced to continue the medication.

Hypochondriasis

Like anxiety, hypochondriasis can be a symptom of depression. When this is the case, depressed people become focused on bodily complaints, and they sometimes deny that they feel depressed or even sad. If they respond well to mood elevating drugs, chances are good that depression is the real problem.

Then there are people who have been in the habit of complaining about their physical ailments throughout their lives. They may have been raised in homes where it wasn't acceptable to express their feelings directly. As a consequence, they may have learned early on that the only effective way to get attention and compassion was to complain that they didn't feel well.

When people who have hypochondriacal tendencies get into their later years and have a lot of time on their hands (and plenty of genuine aches and pains as well), they sometimes become preoccupied with physical problems that don't exist or that are trivial. What they may actually be worried about is dying, but they may be concentrating on their physical symptoms in order to avoid the more disturbing notion of death. Or they may be using their imagined ailments as a way of receiving the attention and physical contact that they crave but aren't getting.

Actual medical problems always should be ruled out when people complain about specific symptoms, and this should be done even if there's a suspicion that they may be imagining things. If nothing is found to be physically wrong with them, they can sometimes be helped if they're willing to participate in therapy. A good therapist can teach them how to get what they need from others in more constructive ways.

In extreme cases of hypochondriasis, people are totally convinced that something terrible is wrong with them. This belief can't be swayed by any amount of medical testing or reassurance by doctors. They go from one physician to another, chronically dissatisfied with the treatment that they're getting and unwilling to confront the psychological aspects of their behavior. This can be time-consuming and frustrating for health care providers and expensive for the health care system. It can also be dangerous because some hypochondriacs undergo unnecessary diagnostic tests, useless treatments, and risky exploratory surgeries. And when they develop real illnesses, their problems are often missed because their physicians have stopped taking the complaints seriously. It's very difficult to get these people into treatment because they're sure that the real issue is the incompetence of the medical establishment.

Substance Abuse

Substance abuse isn't considered to be an emotional disturbance in and of itself, but it certainly affects people's mental health. This problem is thought to be at least as prevalent among older people as it is among the general population.

Alcohol abusers usually begin to drink because it's a socially acceptable way to feel good. And although older people rarely use street drugs because they aren't part of the drug culture, they can and do abuse addictive drugs that have been prescribed to them by their doctors for pain or for anxiety.

Some people who use alcohol and who take addictive drugs develop a tolerance for these substances. Soon they begin to require more and more of the substances in order to achieve the effect that they feel they need. And to complicate matters further, some people are believed to have an inherited biological predisposition to chemical addiction.

Alcohol, of course, is readily available to anyone who wants it. In fact, many stores will deliver it to those who can't get out. Prescription drugs are more difficult to get, but with a little ingenuity they can be obtained. People who abuse them often seek out multiple doctors and use several different pharmacies.

Substance abuse isn't always easily detected in older people. Because many of them don't drive, they're less likely to be picked up by the authorities for driving under the influence. And because most of them don't work, no one notices the fact that they're late to the office or that they're unproductive on the job. Moreover, some of the common signs of substance abuse, such as poor memory, confusion, impaired judgment, angry outbursts, unsociability, falling, poor appetite, and incontinence, often are mistaken for what many people believe are normal problems of old age.

Sometimes the family members, friends, and physicians of an older substance abuser are aware of the situation, but they don't do anything about it. They may be afraid that they'll insult or anger her. They may figure that because she doesn't have long to live, she should be allowed to enjoy the habit. They may not be aware that effective treatment is available. They may prefer to support the substance abuse because it keeps her quiet and congenial instead of disagreeable and quarrelsome. Or they may hope that the abuse will hasten her death.

Sometimes family members and doctors are substance abusers themselves, and they prefer not to point any fingers. In families where there has been a history of substance abuse, there's often a pact of silence or denial that allows the behavior to continue unchallenged.

It's not always easy to get substance abusers into treatment, but unless they're terminally ill and close to death, it's virtually always worth it to do so. And if they're driving or doing anything else that has the potential to do harm to themselves or others, it's imperative that they get help. Long-standing substance abuse can cause malnutrition and irreversible damage to various organs of the body and it eventually can cause death.

Over the next few weeks, Jan felt apprehensive every time she picked up the phone to call her mother. All she heard were the same endless complaints about the unfairness of the eviction. Roslyn just couldn't seem to get beyond this.

Jan tried every tactic she could think of. She tried compassion, anger, attempts at rational discussion, and even the silent treatment. But absolutely nothing she said or did seemed to have any effect on her mother's attitude.

Jan's sister also talked to their mother regularly, and she wasn't having any luck either. Roslyn remained convinced that her situation was hopeless.

Some Other Problems That Should Be Ruled Out

When older people act as though they have a mental health problem, it may be that something else altogether is going on.

First of all, there are a number of medical conditions that should be ruled out. For example, people with low thyroid blood levels sometimes act depressed, and they occasionally hallucinate as well; and people with high thyroid blood levels sometimes act anxious.

Dementia is another condition that's sometimes mistaken for an emotional problem, particularly for depression. Like depressed people, demented people lose their ability to concentrate and to remember things, and they also tend to stop taking care of themselves. It should be kept in mind, however, that actual depression can occur in the early stages of dementia when people first learn that they're becoming demented. In such cases, when the depression is treated, these people's cognitive abilities often will improve a little along with their moods.

Another situation that's often mistaken for an emotional problem is the misuse of medication. This is one of the leading causes of reversible health problems in the elderly. The reasons why people misuse medication are varied. Their memories may be poor. They may like to experiment with nonprescription drugs while they're taking prescription medication. They may figure that if one pill is good, two might be better. They may be taking medication that has been prescribed for someone else. Or they may go to more than one physician, and each doctor may prescribe drugs for the same problem.

In addition to all of these possibilities, people sometimes don't buy the medication that their physician prescribes for them because the drugs cost too much. Or they don't take their medication because they aren't happy with the way it affects them. And they don't tell their doctor about either of these things. Then, when they don't show any improvement, their doctor may prescribe a different medication or something stronger. This new medication may be too potent for them, and it may have a bad effect on them.

Physicians too are sometimes partly to blame for their older patients' drug misuse. Sometimes doctors prescribe drugs to elderly people when they're not as knowledgeable as they should be about how older bodies absorb, store, break down, and excrete drugs. Sometimes they prescribe one drug to counter the side effects of another medication instead of changing the original dose, finding a better drug, or eliminating it altogether. And sometimes they automatically refill prescriptions without evaluating whether or not there's still a need for the drug.

And finally, some medications can affect people in such a way that they act as though they're mentally unstable. For example, some of the drugs given for high blood pressure can cause depression as a side effect. And decongestants, diet pills, prednisone, cortisone, and some antidepressants can cause anxiety.

One morning, Roslyn's neighbor called Jan and told her that she hadn't seen Roslyn around the building very much and that she was worried about her. Jan, too, was becoming quite concerned and the neighbor's call was enough to prompt her to drive up to see her mother.

When Jan knocked on her mother's door, she got no answer, so she let herself in with her own key. As soon as she walked in, it was immediately clear to her that things weren't right. It was late in the morning, and her mother was still in her nightclothes and in bed. The shades were drawn, no lights were on, and there were cracker boxes and crumbs on the night table. Jan asked her mother what in the world was going on.

Roslyn burst into tears.

Jan was taken aback. She couldn't remember ever seeing her mother cry before, and it frightened her.

When your parent appears to be troubled and un-happy, you may not know where to turn. You want her to find peace and happiness, but this may seem to be an impossibly elusive goal.

The Bottom Line

When you're worried about your parent's mental health, you shouldn't assume that nothing can be done. Help is always available.

Mental health problems may seem as though they're less urgent than physical problems, but you should keep in mind that their effects are just as real. Just as your mother shouldn't have to hurt because of physical pain, she shouldn't have to suffer from emotional pain. And contrary to what you may think, older people have just as much potential to respond to treatment as younger people have. It's well worth it to overcome your reluctance to step in and to make sure that your mother gets the help that she needs.

How to Get Help for Your Parent

If Your Mother Has Been Through a Difficult Loss, Allow Her to Grieve

It may make you uncomfortable to be around your mother when she's sad, but you should keep in mind that emotions are part of life and that she needs to grieve if she has been through a significant loss. Instead of trying to cheer her up, you'll be much more helpful if you acknowledge to her that she's going through a tough time. You can help her by giving her the opportunity to talk about her feelings. If she can express her grief, she'll feel less weighed down, and it will be easier for her to recover and move on.

If she doesn't seem to be getting any better, she might benefit from a bereavement group or from counseling. Protracted grief is one of many mental health problems that responds well to psychotherapy.

If Your Parent Seems to Have an Emotional Problem, See to It That She Gets a Thorough Medical Evaluation

If your mother's problem has been going on for longer than you think it should, if it seems to be getting worse, or if it's interfering with her normal functioning, she should see her primary care physician as a first step. He'll take a history, do a physical exam, and order lab tests to rule out various medical conditions.

He also should review all of her medications to make sure that the drugs and the dosages that she's taking are appropriate. If any of them are causing her to feel depressed or anxious, he can adjust the dosage or prescribe a different drug. And if he suspects that she isn't taking her medication properly, he can educate her about this problem, or he can arrange for a home health agency to check on her for a while.

If the doctor believes that your mother is suffering from an emotional disturbance, he may prescribe medication for it, or he may refer her to a psychiatrist who has more experience with these kinds of drugs. Another possibility is that he may refer her to another kind of mental health professional for psychotherapy.

If he suspects that her problem is substance abuse, he may choose to deal with it himself, or he may refer her to an appropriate treatment program.

If Your Parent Is Willing and Able to Participate in Psychotherapy, Encourage Her to Do So

Psychotherapy is one of the best ways to get to the root of an emotional problem. Just because your mother isn't so young anymore, you shouldn't assume that she's too inflexible to get into therapy or that she's insufficiently insightful to benefit from it. What's important is that she believes that the process might help her and that she's willing to share her feelings with a therapist. Her chances of profiting from therapy are greater if she finds a therapist with whom she's comfortable and who enjoys working with elderly patients.

Psychotherapy can be a real boon for older people. In addition to helping them resolve their problems, it forces them to get out of the house, it encourages them to stay connected to the real world, it gives them intellectual stimulation, and it provides an opportunity for socialization.

If Your Parent's Problem Is Drug Misuse, Do What You Can to Prevent It

One way you can help your mother prevent drug misuse is to get her a divided pill box in which her pills can be laid out a week in advance and can be organized by day and by time. These boxes are available at most pharmacies. Another thing you can do is to go through her medicine, throw out all outdated drugs, and put away any still current medication that she's not presently taking. And it may also be a good idea for her to patronize a single pharmacy so that the pharmacist can spot dangerous situations such as two physicians prescribing drugs for her for the same condition.

If the misuse continues, it no longer may be possible for your mother to manage her own medicine.

If Your Parent's Emotional Problems Persist, Get a Referral to a Psychiatrist

If your mother isn't already seeing a psychiatrist and if a reasonable amount of time has passed and the treatment that she's receiving doesn't seem to be working, you should consider asking her doctor to refer her to one. A geriatric psychiatrist would be a good choice, particularly if your mother is suffering from dementia or other health problems in addition to her emotional difficulties.

Psychiatrists have the full arsenal of treatments available to them. They can prescribe drugs and do psychotherapy, some of them can administer electroconvulsive therapy, and they can admit patients to psychiatric facilities.

Hospitalization usually is done as a last resort, but there are times when it has real value. It can be useful when people have medical problems that aren't easily separated from their psychological problems and when it's important to monitor the effects of medication. It's also a good choice for people who need a safe place for detoxification, who aren't able to care for themselves, or who are dangerous to themselves or to others. Getting a seriously disturbed person out of the home can be a godsend for overstressed and exhausted families that desperately need a break.

In some situations, day hospitalization is a very good option.

Do What You Can to Help Your Parent Reduce Stress in Her Life

There are some things you can do that will help your mother achieve as much control over her life as possible. If she feels that she's in control, her life will be less stressful. You can help her set up a daily and weekly routine in such a way that she can accomplish all of the things that she wants to do without becoming overwhelmed. But try to see to it that her goals are realistic so that she isn't experiencing constant frustration. You also can encourage her to use any special equipment that might make it easier for her to manage independently at home. And finally, you can assist her in hiring any help that she needs.

If she's still feeling overwhelmed, you might want to suggest to her that she consider moving to a group living situation where many responsibilities will be handled for her.

Help Your Parent Find Ways That She can be Active, Feel Useful, and Get Involved with Others

Most likely, some of your mother's friends and family members have died or moved away, and she may be feeling lonelier and more isolated than she ever has before. As a consequence, she may be preoccupied with herself, she may feel unconnected with other people, and she may lack a sense of purpose.

She may do better if she gets involved in an outside activity that she enjoys. This could be something that has given her pleasure in the past, or it could be something entirely new. She could take her noon meal at a local senior center, she could join a walking club, or she could take an adult education class. Or if she can't or won't go out, she could hire a cleaning person who would provide her with some companionship in addition to some help with the cleaning.

One of the best ways for people to become less self-absorbed is to help others. Perhaps you can think of some things that your mother can do to help you or your other family members. She can take care of your pet when you're out of town, she can take the grandchildren to a matinee at the theater, or she can write down some old family recipes.

Or perhaps she'd be interested in doing volunteer work. Even if she's confined to bed, she might be able to make a daily call to someone who lives alone to make sure that he or she is all right. In every community there are dozens of organizations that need volunteers.

Encourage Your Parent to Get Regular Exercise

Exercise alone won't cure your mother's mental health problem, but it can be an important part of a comprehensive treatment plan, and it has been shown to help people in many ways. It strengthens the heart, increases lung capacity, lowers blood pressure, protects against adult-onset diabetes, strengthens bones, stretches and strengthens muscles, keeps joints flexible, helps prevent constipation, increases energy, builds stamina, helps control weight, improves sleep, and reduces tension and anxiety. In addition to all this, research has shown that it releases endorphins in the brain that give people a feeling of well-being.

Your mom should discuss any new exercise regimen with her doctor, and she should start slowly. Most communities have special adapted exercise programs for older people.

Take Any Suicide Threats Seriously

Older people sometimes talk about getting their affairs in order and about making funeral plans. This is an appropriate way for them to have some control over their lives and to get ready for their deaths. But if they seem depressed or despairing when they talk about these things, this can be a cause for concern.

Any suicide threats should be taken seriously when they're made by anyone, but these kinds of warnings are especially worrisome when they're made by elderly people. When they talk about killing themselves, they're usually not trying to manipulate others or get attention. Often their intent truly is to die.

If your mother makes a suicide threat, you should let her physician know about it. And if you feel that the situation is urgent, you should contact your local psychiatric emergency team. The number is usually in the front of the phone book in the emergency listings.

If Your Parent Has a Problem with Substance Abuse, Make Sure That She Gets into Treatment

Once in a while, education about alcohol or drug abuse is enough to convince people to stop. When people learn that the tremors and the unpleasant feelings of anxiety that they experience when they haven't had a drink or a pill in a while are in fact symptoms of substance withdrawal, they may be motivated to quit on their own. And sometimes, all that's necessary is for a medical professional to broach the subject openly with them and to break the pact of silence. But most of the time, people need to get into some sort of treatment program.

Every community has resources that provide counseling, education, information, and referrals for substance abuse. You can look in the yellow pages of the phone book under alcohol or drug treatment to find out what programs are available in your parents' area. Many of them are covered by private health insurance and by Medicare.

Jan finally realized that something must be desperately wrong with her mother. She sat down on the bed next to Roslyn, tried to comfort her, and told her that she thought she'd better spend the night.

Her mother nodded silently.

Jan got her mother into the shower and back into a clean bed. Then she ran to the market for some groceries and made her a hot meal. As she straightened up around the place, Jan noticed that there was moldy food in the fridge, and she discovered that her mother hadn't gone down to get her mail for several days.

After Roslyn fell asleep, Jan called her sister and told her what had happened. Her sister was just as concerned as Jan was and agreed with her that their mother's problem must be much more serious than they'd thought. She told Jan that she wanted to come out as soon as possible to be with them, and Jan thought that sounded like a very good idea.

Recognizing Your Own Limitations

Dealing with your unhappy and troubled mother will not be pleasant, and it may be extremely frustrating for you. Your mother may complain and obsess about the same things over and over, and she may be so self-absorbed that you don't want to be around her.

You can suggest some ways that she can make her life better, and you can get her into competent professional hands; but beyond these things, there is a limit to what you can accomplish. You can't be responsible for her happiness.

However, there are a few things you can do that will make the situation easier on yourself. You can try to refrain from reinforcing her disturbed thinking, and this may reduce it a little. You can respond to the feelings behind her words by trying to get her to focus on what's really bothering her and by giving her positive feedback every time she expresses her feelings appropriately. And you can give her plenty of attention when she talks about other things.

But if you see that you're the one who's becoming depressed or anxious, or if you realize that you're sacrificing your own life because you're overinvolved with your mother's problems, it's time for you to set some limits and to start looking out for yourself.

The next morning, Jan bundled her mother up and brought her to the doctor. They'd have to put off looking for apartments for a while.

▼
Chapter
10

When Your Parent
Is Demented

Shirley was an executive secretary who'd been divorced for many years and whose children were now grown and on their own. Her one great passion in life was contract bridge, and she spent her spare time traveling to tournaments and feverishly accumulating master points. For the past several months however, she'd been so worried about her mother, Eve, that she hadn't been able to concentrate on her bridge game.

At first, Shirley noticed that her mother tended to repeat herself, that she sometimes lost her train of thought in the middle of conversations, and that she occasionally had trouble finding the right word. This bothered Shirley, but she managed to push it out of her mind. Lately however, Eve had seemed unusually apprehensive and quiet, and this alarmed Shirley because her mother was normally an outgoing person.

She shared her concerns with her father, Harry, but he acted a little defensive and insisted that the only thing wrong with Eve was the fact that she was getting on in years. Shirley dearly hoped that he was right.

Then, a few weeks later she got a call from her father. He was obviously quite shaken. One of the neighbors had just come to the

134

door with Eve. The woman had found her wandering around and looking confused. She'd gone to the convenience store down the street and had been unable to find her way back home.

The Lowdown on Dementia

Dementia is the correct medical term for what's often called senility. People are considered demented if they suffer from memory loss and if their thinking and problem-solving capacity is impaired to the extent that they no longer can function independently.

Almost everyone experiences some memory lapses with age, and some people may worry that they're becoming demented when they occasionally forget a name or misplace their keys. But most people eventually recollect the name that they've forgotten, and most people remember what they wanted to do with the keys once they find them. And more importantly, most people continue to go about their everyday lives without serious problems.

Even though the incidence of dementia does increase significantly with age, it's not necessarily a part of the aging process. There's always an underlying organic condition that's causing it, and there are more than 50 such conditions. Some of these can be treated successfully, some will improve slowly on their own, some will remain stable, and some will get worse over time. Although most of these conditions are quite rare, others such as multiple small strokes, infections of the central nervous system, brain trauma, normal pressure hydrocephalus, and certain neurological disorders such as multiple sclerosis are more prevalent. But by far the most common cause of dementia is Alzheimer's disease.

Alzheimer's Disease

Alzheimer's is an organic brain disease that is progressive and irreversible, and it's thought to account for over half of all cases of dementia. Alzheimer's patients can live for years, and they often deteriorate slowly and burden their caretakers enormously. As the disease progresses, they experience confusion and memory loss, a decline in their ability to perform routine tasks, personality changes, and a gradual loss of communication skills. Not only do they forget what they once learned, but they also lose the ability to learn anything new. Eventually they're left completely unable to care for themselves.

A tentative diagnosis of Alzheimer's is arrived at only after all other potential causes for the demented behavior have been ruled out. Unfortunately, a definitive diagnosis can't be made until the patient's brain tissue is examined after death.

Researchers are working on isolating the specific cause or causes of this disease, and they're making efforts to develop treatments that will prevent it, slow it down, or stop its progress. But for now, the only treatment that doctors can offer are drugs that sometimes provide relief for associated problems such as depression, agitation, insomnia, paranoid thinking, and angry or threatening behavior.

If You Think That Your Parent Might be Showing Signs of Dementia

If you're concerned about your parent, you can ask yourself these questions:

Does Your Mom Show Reasonable Judgment?

Does she dress appropriately when it's raining outside? Will she use a cane if she's unsteady on her feet?

Does She Appear to be Well-Oriented?

Does she know approximately what time of day it is? The day of the week? The month? The year? Does she know where she is and what she's doing at any given moment?

Does She Seem to Have Adequate Insight Regarding Her Own Emotions and Behavior as Well as the Behavior of Others?

Is she aware that her angry outbursts are upsetting to her family? Does she recognize that others are worried about her?

Does She Have Any Significant Memory Problems?

Does she remember what happened to her three minutes ago? Yesterday? During the last year? Back in her childhood? (Short-term memory is usually the first to go.)

Does She Express Her Feelings Appropriately?

Have there been any changes in the ways that she characteristically reacts to things? Do her emotions seem to be in line with what's happening to her and around her at the moment? Does she smile or laugh when something is funny? Does she respond appropriately when something sad happens?

If your mother is having new difficulty in any of these broad areas of functioning, she should be evaluated by a physician who has had plenty of experience diagnosing dementing disorders. If her doctor thinks that normal functioning is too much to expect at your mother's advanced age, perhaps your mother ought to see another doctor. You can get names of recommended physicians from your local Alzheimer's Association.

The medical work-up for dementia should include a detailed history, reports from family members and friends (including a description of what your mother used to be like), direct observation of behavior, a review of the drugs that she's taking, a complete physical and neurological examination, and possibly other tests as well.

With dementia, as with any other medical condition that afflicts an elderly person, it doesn't always make sense to make use of every diagnostic procedure just because it's available. If your mother is in the last stages of terminal cancer, for example, it hardly seems reasonable to put her through a long, arduous series of tests in order to look for brain abnormalities. The benefits that might be gained from extensive testing should be weighed against the discomfort, the inconvenience, and the expense that's involved. In general, your mother's age, physical and mental condition, and passion to remain alive should all figure into such a decision. However, anyone who shows signs of dementia should undergo at least a basic evaluation because there's always the possibility that the problem isn't dementia at all.

The Dementia Look-alikes

Dementia Look-alikes outwardly resemble dementia but actually are something else altogether. If your parent appears to be demented, it's important that these conditions be ruled out since many of them do respond well to treatment. By far the most common Dementia Look-alikes are depression and delirium.

Depression is very common among older people, but it's often not recognized as such because family members, friends, and even physicians sometimes wrongly believe that it's perfectly natural for the elderly to slow down, to lose their ability to concentrate and think, and to become less interested in the world around them.

Delirium is caused by toxins that affect brain metabolism. Its most distinctive features are its rapid onset and its fluctuation over the course of a day. Almost any physical illness can bring on delirium when an individual is already in a weakened state. Some of the major causes of this condition in older people are drug reactions, alcohol intoxication or withdrawal, metabolic disorders due to fluid imbalance or malnutrition, burns, extreme heat or cold, and the aftereffects of anesthesia. Suspicious symptoms should be investigated right away because delirium can lead to permanent brain damage or death.

After Eve got lost, Shirley knew that they had to bring her in to see the doctor. Harry, too, sadly admitted that something must be wrong.

Eve herself didn't see any reason for going, but Shirley and Harry reminded her that it had been a long time since she'd had a checkup, so she agreed to go if it was so important to them.

The doctor listened to the family's reports, examined Eve, and scheduled her for tests that took the better part of two weeks. When the tests were completed, the doctor called the three of them into her office. She told them that she could find no correctable abnormalities, but she explained to them that because of Eve's behavioral changes, she appeared to be in the early stages of a condition that slowly was affecting her brain.

All three of them were upset to hear this, and Shirley asked a number of questions that the doctor answered as best she could. But it was obvious that for Eve's problem, medicine didn't have many answers.

On the way home, Eve repeatedly told Shirley and Harry how sorry she was. All they could do was assure her that it wasn't her fault, that they loved her, that they'd take good care of her, and that they'd make sure that she'd get the best treatment available.

Later on, when Shirley called the doctor to ask a few follow-up questions, the doctor told her that she suspected that Eve's problem was Alzheimer's Disease. This, of course, had been Shirley's worst fear.

If the medical evaluation indicates that your parent is demented and that nothing can be done about it, you may be faced with a long, hard road ahead. Although some demented people become more or less pleasantly confused, many of them become difficult to deal with, and they can present considerable problems for their family members who often go through years of emotional strain and financial sacrifice.

Whether you're the full-time caregiver for your parent or not, this won't be an easy time for you. There will be moments when you'll lose your temper. There will be days when you'll think you can't go on anymore. And there will be times when you'll feel cheated, trapped, and resentful that you've been dealt a crummy hand.

However, you *can* reduce the wear and tear on yourself.

The Bottom Line

A diagnosis of irreversible dementia is definitely bad news. But, you can make the best of a difficult situation if you accept things as they are and if you use every trick you can.

How to Deal with Your Demented Parent

These suggestions relate specifically to people with Alzheimer's disease, but most of them apply just as well to any demented person.

See to it That Both of Your Parents Have Their Affairs in Order

If there are any important legal or financial matters that your parents haven't taken care of, there's no time to lose once the diagnosis of dementia is made. It's especially important that your parents give some thought to long-term financial planning because the parent who's demented could live for many years and could end up requiring extensive (and costly) care.

Help Your Parent to Stay Healthy

If your mother stays in reasonably good health, she'll have fewer problems to cope with. You should do what you can to see to it that she gets proper nutrition, adequate daily exercise, good medical and dental care, and periodic vision and hearing evaluations (and corrections if necessary).

Be Aware of Safety

You and your other family members will have to decide which activities your mom can do independently, which ones she can do with supervision, and which ones she should avoid altogether. (Very risky activities, such as driving, are out of the question.) As her dementia progresses, you'll have to continue making judgment calls. Eventually you may have to hide sharp items and keys, and you may have to remove knobs from stoves and put locks on certain drawers, cabinets, and doors. Your mother should wear an identification bracelet as a precautionary measure in case she wanders away from home, and recent photos of her should be on hand to show the police and put in the newspaper if necessary.

Get Help

Keep in mind that no one can care for a demented person alone. Caregivers should always share the responsibility with others, they should take breaks from time to time, and they should continue to live their own lives as fully as possible. If you're doing much of the caregiving for your mother, you need to be on the lookout for signs that things are getting out of hand. This is one time when she needs you to be healthy and strong and when you need to take good care of yourself.

If you're having trouble dealing with the situation, you might want to consider getting some counseling for yourself, or you might want to join a support group for caregivers of demented people. Your local Alzheimer's Association should be able to connect you with a group in your area. You'll probably get some practical tips from the other members of the group, but even more important, you'll get reassurance that you're not alone and that others are going through the same kinds of experiences and are sharing the same kinds of feelings that you are.

It had been two full years since Eve was diagnosed, and she'd deteriorated considerably in that time. Her personality had lost its sparkle, she had a worried look on her face most of the time, and she asked a lot of repetitive, anxious questions. She and Harry rarely went out socially anymore, and their friends hardly ever stopped by or had them over.

The hardest thing for Harry to deal with was Eve's short attention span. She'd put a cake in the oven and then totally forget about it. She'd start up the vacuum cleaner, and leave it running when she felt compelled to see if the mail had arrived. Harry would find melted ice cream in the closet, dish towels in the oven, and burnt pots in the cupboards. His entire day was spent picking up after Eve, and by the time evening came around, he was exhausted.

Shirley was worried that the strain was affecting her father's health. For months she'd been trying to get him to put her mother into a day-care program, but he was determined to care for her himself. Shirley was spending all her spare time helping him out. The last time she'd been to a bridge tournament was when her sister came to stay with their folks a few months earlier. She had no life of her own anymore.

Finally, she told her father that she admired his devotion, but if he didn't get Eve into a day-care program, he'd soon have two demented women to care for instead of one.

Encourage Your Parent to Lead as Normal a Life as Possible

Your mother will do better if she's allowed to continue to take part in her customary activities for as long as she can. Whenever possible, she should be included in social gatherings, and she should be encouraged to go on pursuing any hobbies or interests that she enjoyed in the past.

Activities that would only result in failure or frustration should be avoided, but adjustments often can be made so that she can do many things herself. If paying the bills has become too complicated, she may still be able to sign the checks and put them in the envelopes. If she'd like to prune the bushes but you're afraid that this could lead to a disaster, you might suggest that she tackle the hoeing instead.

Give Your Parent Opportunities to Make Choices

Your mom should continue to exercise her judgment and make as many choices for herself as is feasible. This will help her retain a sense of dignity and will allow her to feel that she still has some control over her life. When she's only mildly demented, she may be able to decide what she'd like to wear for the day. As she becomes more seriously impaired, she may only be able to choose between two preselected outfits. And eventually, she may find it too confusing to make any choice at all, but she can still be shown the outfit that's been selected for her, and she can be told how pretty she'll look in it.

Try to Provide a Quiet, Calm Environment for Your Parent

Your mom will cooperate better and she'll be less belligerent if she isn't exposed to a lot of noise and confusion. Large crowds, rambunctious children, and loud music may be too much for her to handle. She's already confused as it is. Overstimulating her may only make her agitated and upset.

Set up a Predictable Daily Routine

Your mom will be more relaxed and more compliant if her meals, baths, walks, and other activities take place at the same times each day. And she'll probably do better if each activity is done exactly the same way each time. This applies especially to activities that aren't particularly enjoyable such as taking medication or being diapered.

Give Your Parent Plenty of Time to Do Things

Give your mom extra time to perform even the simplest task. If you rush her, you'll only create frustration for everyone. A meal that used to take her 20 minutes to eat may now take her more than an hour. If you choose to stay at the table with her, you should find something that will keep you busy so that you won't become impatient.

Keep Surprises to a Minimum

Your mom will be easier to deal with if she's confronted with as few surprises as possible. To avoid frightening her, you should approach her from the front so she can see you, and you should speak calmly to her as you do so. If she's in a wheelchair, you shouldn't move her without telling her first. Even though she may not understand everything you're saying, you can still talk to her as if she does understand. As you feed her, for example, you can tell her what she's eating. If nothing else, the familiarity of your voice may comfort her.

Communicate in Every Way You Can

Your mom will stay independent longer and she'll cooperate better with you if you explain everything to her in simple language. To get the message across more effectively, you can demonstrate what you're saying, you can write it down, and you can even draw her a picture.

If she needs to wipe off her feet before going into the house, you can do it yourself as you talk her through each step. If she gets lost around the house, you can put up signs with words and pictures on all of the doors to remind her which room is which. You can also label cabinets and drawers so that she'll know where to find things.

Break Activities Down into Simple Steps

As your mom's short-term memory becomes increasingly impaired, she may have great difficulty with tasks that involve a series of actions. But if each activity is broken down into individual steps, and if each step is presented to her one at a time, she may be able to perform the steps on her own. Getting dressed may be too complicated for her if she has to do it from beginning to end. But if you hand her one item of clothing at a time, she may still be able to manage the job.

Respond to the Feelings Behind Your Parent's Words

Don't try to argue with your mom when her thoughts are confused. You'll be much more effective with her if you try to figure out what feelings she's attempting to express and then acknowledge that you understand what she's feeling.

If she announces that she wants to make a phone call to her deceased mother, you don't have to be logical and point out that grandma has been dead for years. Instead, you can agree that it would be nice to talk to grandma and that you wonder what she'd like to tell her.

If she kicks the bed and yells at the nonexistent cats to get off of it, you don't have to argue with her about whether or not the cats exist. Instead, you can tell her that you see how angry she is and that you'd like to know what could be done to make things better.

Find Creative Ways to Head off Repetitive Questions

Your mom may repeat herself often because she has lost her short-term memory, so try to remember that she's not repeating things on purpose to aggravate you. If you find this habit annoying (and most people do), you can experiment with a few techniques that might help.

If she continually asks you if it's time to visit the doctor yet, you can try to get her involved in a conversation or an activity that might distract her. Or you can get an index card and write DOCTOR APPOINTMENT IS AT TWO and draw a clock with its hands indicating two o'clock, and you can give it to her to hold. Or you can try to avoid the questions altogether by telling her about the appointment only when you're actually ready to leave.

Use Ingenuity as You Deal with Difficult Behavior Problems

You won't be able to reason with your mother but you may be able to think up some clever strategies that will help prevent annoying behavior problems. If she tries to undress in public, you can dress her in clothes that fasten from behind. If she talks gibberish all day long, you can wear earphones and listen to music when you're around her. If she bangs her cane constantly, you can wrap foam rubber around the tip of it to muffle the noise and to protect the furniture.

See If Medication Will Help

In general, medication should be used to control behavior only when other approaches have failed, because many drugs have undesirable side effects. But if your efforts at ingenuity haven't panned out and your mom's behavior is creating a significant problem, see if her doctor can prescribe medication to control it. If she doesn't respond to one drug, she may respond better to another. You can help the doctor by keeping records of the times she gets her medication, the dosages given to her, and any behavioral changes you observe.

Let Yourself Enjoy the Lighter Moments

It may not be easy for you to maintain your sense of humor in the face of longstanding stress, but doing so can help you keep things in perspective and it can allow you to let off steam. When you're out of your mother's earshot, you can laugh with your sister about the time your mother took her false teeth out at the dinner table and buttered them.

In addition, you should appreciate the moments when your mother will reveal small glimmers of her past personality such as a particular brand of humor, a characteristic facial expression, or a private signal that only another family member would understand. Although such moments can be painful reminders of the drastic changes that have taken place, they can also help you keep going when you're feeling discouraged.

Another 18 months had gone by, and the day-care center that Eve attended during the week turned out to be a blessing. After she started going there, Harry was much more relaxed and better rested, and Shirley felt as if a weight had been lifted from her shoulders.

But during the past few weeks, Eve had become increasingly difficult to handle at home. She spent much of her time pacing back and forth and getting into things. Even though Harry put locks on many of the drawers and cabinets, he'd still find her pulling tissues out of the box one by one or picking the leaves off a plant. He couldn't leave her unsupervised for a moment.

One evening Harry called Shirley and told her that he couldn't take it anymore. Earlier that day he'd brought Eve to the lobby to pick up their mail, and when he turned around, he saw that she'd urinated all over the floor.

The next day Shirley and her dad visited several nursing homes. The one they selected for Eve was bigger than they'd have liked, it wasn't as close by as they'd have preferred, and it cost more than Harry could really afford. But it was the one that felt best to them.

Harry was heartbroken when he had to tell Eve that she'd be leaving her home, but he felt even worse when he realized that she didn't seem to care.

It will be difficult for you to watch as your parent becomes increasingly demented, yet it is possible for some good to come out of such an unfortunate experience.

Sometimes it can happen that the personality changes brought on by dementia are actually for the better. Someone who used to be cold and unloving can become warm and affectionate, or someone who used to be critical and demanding can become more peaceful and accepting. This doesn't mean that dementia is ever something to be wished for, but these kinds of positive changes can soften the blow a little.

Furthermore, sometimes tragedies like this can bring family members closer together. As you get involved in the caregiving, you'll feel good about yourself as you rise to the occasion. And you may amaze yourself with your resourcefulness and resilience.

It had been a year since Eve had moved into the nursing home, and she didn't recognize her family anymore. She'd stopped speaking altogether, and she spent her days shuffling up and down the halls.

Shirley came by to see her mother once a week, and the two of them often took a walk outside. One afternoon as they walked arm in arm, Shirley absentmindedly hummed "Oh Susanna" to herself. Her mother had sung it to her often when Shirley was very little.

Suddenly out of the blue, Eve chimed in, ". . . with a banjo on my knee."

Shirley stopped, gave her mother a sidelong look, and smiled. Then she walked on and hummed as Eve shuffled along beside her.

▼

Chapter

11

When Your Parent Must Be in a Nursing Home

Kathleen *had never married, and for the past ten years she'd been living with her widowed mother, Mary, who suffered from advanced emphysema.*

Mary could walk only short distances, and she spent her days and nights in a reclining chair with her upper body elevated so that she could breathe. Aside from her daughter, Mary's only companion was her parakeet, and her only visitors were her other children and her pastor.

Mary wasn't an easy lady to live with. She was bossy and stubborn, and she coughed nonstop. Kathleen's brothers and sisters couldn't understand how Kathleen put up with her. They'd tried to convince her to put their mother into a nursing home, but Kathleen was opposed to the idea. Because she was the oldest child and the only one without family responsibilities, it seemed only right to her that she care for their mother. And as long as she could go to work and get out to a movie or go bowling once in a while, she was willing to do it.

But the situation deteriorated when Mary came down with a bad case of the flu. After she recovered, she was much weaker than she'd been before. She couldn't get up from her chair without help and no longer could do her own breathing treatments. Someone had to be with her constantly.

Because of this, Kathleen reluctantly acknowledged that the time finally had come to put her mother into a nursing home.

Why Nursing Home Placement Is So Hard

The decision to place a parent in a nursing home is one of the most difficult ones that adult children have to make. People almost always regard the move as something to be avoided at all costs, and most older people see nursing homes as the end of the road. From early on, many parents tell their children that—no matter what—they never want to be put into such a place.

Other kinds of living situations may not be considered ideal, but they're not regarded with outright fear the way that nursing homes are. Even if the stay is intended to be short, nursing home residents and their families are still often apprehensive about it. Many people have the attitude that those who must be in nursing homes no longer have a real role or purpose in the world, that they're being warehoused until they die.

If you're thinking about placing your mother in a nursing home, you're probably anxious about how she's going to adjust, and you're probably worried about the quality of the care that she'll receive. You may also be afraid of what others will think of you because you're not making the necessary sacrifices that would enable her to stay home. And you may feel frustrated that there isn't a better solution available.

But the reality is that the time for nursing home placement can come for anyone. For this reason, you should never threaten your parent with placement in a nursing home, because some day you may really have to put her into a home, and it won't help matters if she feels she's being punished. And similarly, you shouldn't promise her that you'll never, ever, under any circumstances, put her into a nursing home because at some point down the line you may have to do exactly that.

The decision to place your parent in a nursing home is usually an agonizing one because it confirms two painful facts. The first is the fact that she has deteriorated to the extent that she can't care for herself. And the second is the fact that you're unable or unwilling to do what's necessary to care for her yourself. Still, the decision to follow through on placement is much easier in some cases than it is in others.

If your mom is severely demented and if she needs round-the-clock attention, it's possible for her to be cared for at home. But the house would have to be converted into a hospital-like setting with 24-hour nursing help. For most people, such an arrangement would be thoroughly impractical (and also prohibitively expensive). So in situations like this, nursing home placement is almost always the only realistic option.

But chances are good that your mother's situation won't be quite so clear-cut, and in order to come to a decision, you'll probably have to take three things into account. The first consideration is the level of physical care she requires, the second is her personality, and the third is the amount of caregiving time that you and the rest of your family are willing to put in.

If two people have the same physical care needs, the unappreciative, demanding, uncooperative one probably will end up in a nursing home sooner than will the sweet-natured, accommodating, responsive one. And whereas one caregiver may be willing to manage virtually all of the necessary care for someone without feeling unduly burdened, another caregiver may feel completely overwhelmed by that much responsibility.

When there's no way for you to pull off a care plan for your mother in her own home, when living under the same roof with her is out of the question, and when her needs are too complicated to be handled in another kind of living situation that offers a lesser level of care, a nursing home may be the only alternative

Kathleen was afraid to tell her mother about her decision because she knew how badly Mary would react. But Kathleen's brothers and sisters kept the pressure on her, and with their help, she finally pulled together enough courage to say the words as gently as she could.

And sure enough, Mary was horrified. In her raspy voice, she asked her children how they could do this to her and bitterly announced that she might as well be dead.

As soon as she heard her mother's reaction, Kathleen started to waver. She doubted that her mother would ever agree to go. But her siblings stepped in and reminded her that there was no doubt that she was doing the right thing. One of them suggested that it might be a good idea to ask the pastor to speak with their mother. Kathleen agreed, and called him right away.

The pastor stopped by later that day and had a long, private talk with Mary. Kathleen held her breath during the entire time he was in her room. When he finally emerged, she was relieved to hear that her mother had given word that she'd go along with the decision. Mary made it clear, however, that she was not at all happy about it.

Choosing a Good Nursing Home for Your Particular Parent

When you look around and learn more about the world of nursing homes, you'll discover that they're certainly far from perfect. But once you get used to the idea, you'll also come to realize that many of them are making a genuine effort to do the best job they can.

As you begin your search, you can get a list of homes from the licensing division of your state health department, but your best bet is to consult with a Pro Who Knows the Ropes. The Pro should be able to suggest some specific homes that might be particularly well-suited to your parent and may be able to steer you toward the ones that have a reputation for giving reasonably good care.

You should also check with your parent's doctor to see if there are any places that he or she can recommend. Physicians usually make it a practice to see residents at only a limited number of nursing homes in their area so that they won't spend their time driving all over town. If you select a home that your mother's doctor doesn't go to, she'll have to switch to a physician who does go to that facility.

Finally, you can talk to other people who have some experience with the nursing homes in your mother's area. However, you need to be sure that the information they're giving you is current because there may have been changes in ownership and staff, and the quality of care may have changed as well. Remember also that people often respond differently to the same set of circumstances, and so you should see the places for yourself before you make any judgments.

When you've narrowed the possibilities down to a short list, you should go ahead and visit the facilities. Then go back and revisit the top contenders, but at a different time of day so that you can get a more complete picture.

As you consider a nursing home, there are a few important questions you should ask yourself. Is the location of the facility convenient for visiting? Are the residents out of their beds when it's appropriate for them to be up and about? Are they neatly groomed? Do they appear to be comfortable? Is the place clean and odor-free? Are activities available that would be of interest to your parent? Does the monthly meal menu have enough variety? Do the staff members interact in a gentle, respectful way with the people whom they're hired to take care of?

153

One home may be more appropriate for your parent than another. Some are very large and offer a wide variety of activities. Others are smaller and have more of a family feeling. Some place more emphasis on rehabilitation than others do. Some are more luxurious than others. Some are located in bustling cities where there are plenty of people-watching opportunities outside. Others are situated in more tranquil rural settings. And some are affiliated with particular religious groups or cater to specific populations, such as retired teachers.

Cost varies some, too, but the fact is that nursing home care is always expensive. People usually are astonished to discover that Medicare will pay for it only under very specific circumstances and then only for a limited period of time. Some people have their own nursing home insurance, which covers a part or all of the cost, and others have Medicaid coverage, which will pay for all of the cost; but many people must pay for nursing home care out of their own pockets.

If your mother is going to be in a nursing home for any significant length of time, and if she's going to be paying for it herself, the person in the nursing home who handles finances should be able to go over financial options with you and your parent. You may also want to speak to a financial consultant with expertise in this field.

Kathleen felt terrible about what she was doing, but she forced herself to go with one of her sisters to visit several nursing homes in their area. Her sister brought along a video camera and filmed a few scenes at each place so that their mother could have a say in the selection process.

As they were being shown around the first home, Kathleen became even more depressed; but after they'd seen a few more places, the first one didn't seem so bad after all.

That evening they tried to get Mary to watch the video, but she wouldn't even look at it. So Kathleen and her siblings went ahead and made the final choice themselves and arranged to have their mother admitted as soon as possible before she could change her mind.

Two days later, Mary was taken by nonemergency ambulance to her new home. Kathleen prayed that she was doing the right thing.

Making the Adjustment

Sometimes when people enter nursing homes, they're oblivious to the fact that there has been a change in their environment. But if your mother is aware of what's happening to her, she'll probably be quite apprehensive about the move. For most elderly people, getting used to any new living situation is never easy no matter how pleasant a place it is. But adjusting to a nursing home is especially difficult.

Your mom will miss her familiar surroundings. She may feel uncomfortable being around other residents who are disturbing to look at and who may be demented. She may have trouble getting used to the noises and the smells. She may not like the food. She may have difficulty adjusting to a regimented daily routine that's different from what she's accustomed to. She may not like having a roommate, and she may complain that she has hardly any privacy. She may have trouble getting used to having strangers help her with intimate activities, such as bathing, toileting, and dressing. She may become annoyed when she doesn't always get the help that she needs at the moment she wants it. It may be hard for her to get used to a changing staff with names and faces that she can't keep straight. And some of these people may not speak English well, which may be an additional source of frustration for her.

For most people, these kinds of issues are significant, and it's not at all unusual for new nursing home residents to become depressed and to repeatedly ask their families why they must be there.

After she moved in, Mary did what she could to make all of her children's lives miserable. She turned away whenever they came into her room, and she spoke to them only in monosyllables.

Kathleen felt the sting of her mother's bitterness more keenly than her siblings did, but she forced herself to visit Mary even though it was unpleasant for her. She'd come in the evenings after work and would try to make small talk, but all Mary did was sulk. After a week of this, Kathleen began to believe that she'd done the wrong thing. She was so upset that she took up smoking after having quit a few years earlier.

Your parent's move to a nursing home probably will not be easy, and you may feel that there's little that you can do to make the situation any better. But that's not the case.

The Bottom Line

Even though a nursing home will never be the same as home, your continued, active involvement in your parent's life *can* make a difference.

How to Help Your Parent Make the Best of Nursing Home Life

Be Honest

You may be afraid to bring up the subject of nursing home placement with your mother because you're concerned that she'll react negatively. So you may be tempted to use a euphemism such as "special care unit" instead of just coming out and telling her where she's really going. Or you may be tempted to lie to her and say that you're putting her in the facility for only a few days until she's strong enough to return home. But you should resist the temptation to say these kinds of things. When she figures out what has actually happened, she'll not only be angry at you, but .it will be hard for her to trust you again.

Also, you shouldn't try to convince her that the placement is for her benefit, because both of you know that this isn't entirely true. And you shouldn't give her phony assurances that everything will be wonderful, because it probably won't be.

Allow Some Time for the Idea to Sink In

When you first mention nursing home placement to your mother, her first reaction may be quite negative. She'll probably need some time to get used to the idea. Give her the opportunity to grieve for the losses that she's going through and to think about the implications of the move. It's natural and necessary that she do this.

Involve Your Parent in the Selection Process

After you've visited several facilities, you can report to your mother on the arguments for and against each one. Then, when possible, you should bring her to visit the top con-.tenders, and you can let her make the final selection. If she isn't able to be involved in the decision, you can share the responsibility with your other family members. This way there will be less likelihood that you'll be singled out for criticism.

Help Make the Transition Less Traumatic

If you can, you should stay with your mom for several hours on her first day in the nursing home. Then you can leave for awhile and come back in the evening to check on her. Tell her when you'll be coming again, and be sure to be on time. She may appreciate having a phone by her bed so that she can call you whenever she wants to.

You should do your best to empathize with her fears and her concerns and to let her know that you understand her anxieties about institutional life. You can share your worries with her too, but try not to frighten her unnecessarily. Let her know how much you appreciate the effort that she's making, and try to concentrate on the positive steps that can be taken to make the move easier on her. The important thing is to reassure her that you'll look out for her well-being.

Let her express her anger, and try to listen to her without becoming defensive. If she's being inappropriately critical, help her identify her feelings and help her find the real cause for her anger. (It could be that she's angry at you for making the move necessary.) Keep in mind that the adjustment period can take long, painful weeks and sometimes months. Physicians sometimes prescribe antidepressant medication or sedatives to help people get through the transition period.

During this time, you may continue to question the wisdom of your decision. But you should remember that you aren't doing your mother any favors if you keep her at home and then end up resenting her for it.

Don't Burn Your Parent's Bridges Sooner Than Necessary

Even if your mom is never expected to return to her former living situation, you should try to keep it intact for a few months. This way she won't feel as though so many losses are occurring at once. When she's settled in the nursing home, you can begin to talk with her about cleaning out her home and giving it up.

Visit Your Parent Regularly

It's extremely important that you visit your mother on a regular basis. This may not be easy for you because each visit may rekindle your feelings of guilt and ambivalence about the placement itself. But every time you go, you're letting her know that you care about her. And just as important, you're letting the staff know that you're watching how she's being treated and that you expect her to receive good care. Even if your mother doesn't recognize you anymore, it's still vital that you go to see her regularly in order to make sure that she's getting the care that she needs.

When you can't visit as often as you'd like to (or think you should), consider asking other family members or friends to help you out. Or perhaps you could hire someone to go in your place.

It's a good idea to establish a routine so that your mom can look forward to your next visit. And when you leave, be sure to let her know when you're coming again.

As her bonds within the facility get stronger, you may not have to come quite as often.

Use Your Visiting Time Well

Think about how you'd like to spend your time with your mother, and use your imagination to come up with activities that you'll both enjoy. What you do with her during your visits will depend on her interests, her general health, and her mental condition. If you're having trouble coming up with ideas, ask the staff or the family members of other residents for some suggestions.

There are all kinds of things you can do. You can take her for a walk in the fresh air. You can share news with her from the outside world. You can tell her funny stories about the kids. You can bring along the kids, or an old friend, or a pet. You can play a game of cards. You can play a musical instrument. You can rub her back, brush her hair, or do her nails. You can bring her tasty treats, colorful and comfortable things to wear, materials for handicrafts, and tapes of her favorite music. You can do a crossword puzzle together. You can thumb through family photo albums or work on a family tree together. You can read her a magazine article. You can look though mail order catalogs or write a letter with her. You can share an occasional meal or attend a special activity in the nursing home with her. You can watch a television program with her or just sit by her and hold her hand. And if she can get out, you can take her out to lunch or bring her to a family function.

Try to involve other residents in your visits if your mom likes this idea. This can help her develop relationships that she can enjoy when you're not there.

Help Make Your Parent's Room as Homelike as Possible

You can encourage your mom to bring along some personal belongings that she'd like to have with her in the nursing home. Because theft and loss can be a problem in any facility, it's not advisable to bring items of considerable monetary or sentimental value. But she certainly can hang up pictures, put out favorite knickknacks, and display photos of family members and artwork done by her grandchildren or great-grandchildren. Even if your mom isn't alert enough to appreciate these things, her room will feel more cheerful when visitors come.

Get to Know the Staff

Working in a nursing home is hard. The pay isn't great, and the conditions frequently are difficult. Yet, some very dedicated individuals make this their career and they do a wonderful job. You should make it your business to get to know the nursing assistants who will provide your mother's daily care, and you also should become acquainted with other key personnel, such as the head nurse, the social worker, the occupational and physical therapists, the activity director, and the dietitian.

Try to let the staff know about it when you think that they're doing a good job. Nursing home residents and their families often notice what staff members aren't doing, but they don't always pay attention to what they *are* doing. When you're grateful for something, thank them and tell them exactly what it is that you appreciate. Giving gifts to individual staff members is usually discouraged, but you can let them know that you appreciate their hard work with a thoughtful note or with a basket of fresh fruit from your tree for all the staff to share.

Respect the Staff When They Tell You That They Can't Do Something

Some of the physical care that your mom receives in the nursing home is ordered by her doctor. The staff may not permit her to go to the bathroom on her own because the doctor has ordered that she be accompanied whenever she gets out of bed. If your mother would like to walk on her own and you see no reason why she shouldn't, you'll need to speak to her physician. If the doctor agrees with you, he or she can modify the orders. Anytime the staff is operating under the doctor's orders, they can't make changes on their own.

Help the Staff See Your Parent as a Real Person

It's a nice idea to let the staff know what your mother was like when she was younger. You can show them pictures of her as she used to be. You can mention that the blanket on her bed is one of the many that she crocheted for her family, that she and your dad were terrific dancers, that she retired from her job as a dog trainer only five years ago, or that she raised seven kids. This kind of personal information will help them see her as an individual rather than as just another old lady. It also will give them something to talk about with her.

Attend Care Planning Meetings If You Can

In some facilities, residents and their family members are invited to attend periodic interdisciplinary care planning meetings. If you have the opportunity to take part in these sessions, you should take advantage of it. During the meetings, both short- and long-term goals are set for your parent, and the staff members discuss how these goals can be best achieved. Everything that's decided at the meeting is written down in your mother's chart that the staff members refer to every day.

Care planning meetings provide an excellent forum for you to straighten out any concerns or misunderstandings that you may have with the staff. They also give you an opportunity to show your mom that you're interested in the programs and services that are available to her. If you can't attend the meetings, you can still discuss your questions and concerns with staff members and try to work things out with them.

Be an Advocate for Your Parent

It will help if you let the staff know about your mom's habits and preferences so that they can give her more personal care. If she likes her coffee cup filled only halfway so that she can put plenty of milk in it, make sure that they know this. Within the limitations of scheduling and staffing, they should be able to take her preferences into account.

When your mom has a complaint, try to personally check it out. If she reports that her breakfast is always cold, come in early one day and see for yourself if this is the case. Then when you know for sure that there's a problem, you can speak up about it.

If the difficulty involves one staff member, you should try to correct the situation by talking directly to that person. Instead of telling her what she's not doing, try to explain to her what you think could be done to solve the problem. You can say something like:

I think you'd find that my mom would be much more cooperative about taking her showers if the room were nice and warm before you got started.

If you're not getting satisfaction or if you have a concern that involves several staff members, you can go to the head nurse, and you can say something like:

Many of the staff people don't seem to realize that my mom is completely alert. It's true that she's deaf, but she can understand people if they take the time to write a short note on her pad of paper.

You should get satisfaction from taking those two steps. But, if you're still not happy, you can go to the facility administrator, and you can say something like:

I've spoken to the head nurse twice about having the windows fixed in my mother's room. She said she reported it to maintenance. Is there some reason why they haven't taken care of the problem in ten days?

And finally, if the problem is still not resolved to your satisfaction, you can call the office of your state's Long-Term Care Ombudsman. This is a federally-mandated service that was created to handle complaints made by nursing home residents and their families. (They do the same thing in regard to other licensed long-term care facilities as well.) You can get their phone number from the administrator of the nursing home, from a Pro, or from the local Area Agency on Aging.

If the Placement Absolutely Isn't Working, Make a Change

Because any change is extremely hard on an elderly person, the right strategy is to put plenty of energy into choosing the best possible nursing home for your mother in the beginning. That way you'll be as confident as you can be that you've made the best choice. Then you should make every effort possible to resolve any problems that come up.

However, if your mom has been in the nursing home for several months and she still isn't feeling reasonably comfortable and settled, if there are legitimate reasons why another facility would be a better fit, or if the care that she's getting has gotten worse, you may need to consider another home. You might also want to think about whether she has improved enough to return to a more independent living arrangement—a happy and often overlooked possibility.

Get Support for Yourself

When you're having your own difficulties adjusting to your mother's nursing home placement, it might help if you speak to some of the family members of other residents in the facility and ask them how they've handled the kinds of issues that you're dealing with. You also might want to consider participating in the support group that many homes organize for family members of their residents. And in addition to these things, you may want to think about getting counseling from a clergyperson or a therapist if you need help in sorting out your feelings.

Because she was so frustrated, Kathleen began attending the weekly family support meetings in the nursing home. When she heard about the kinds of problems that some of the other people were having with their parents, she didn't feel quite so bad. She asked them for some suggestions on how to deal with her mother, and they were full of ideas. She also got tips from some of the staff, and she met a few times with the pastor who gave her a crash course on how to listen to her mother's feelings without becoming defensive. All of these things helped her become more confident in the decision that she had made.

Then Kathleen came up with a plan.

She began to visit Mary on weekend mornings when she was well rested instead of after work when she was exhausted. (She asked her family and the pastor to try to come in on weekdays.) And when she came, she brought along some home-cooked treats, and once in a while she brought her mother's parakeet. When she spoke to Mary, she made a point of telling her that this change must be very hard for her, and she also mentioned that getting the constant cold shoulder was making it extremely unpleasant for her to come to visit.

It's important to keep in mind that having your mom in a nursing home will not solve all your problems. You'll worry about the quality of her care. You'll have occasional doubts about the wisdom of your decision. And you'll still feel tied down and afraid to leave town.

But chances are that you'll eventually adjust. The institutional atmosphere and the sight of all those old people sitting around in wheelchairs that was such a horror to you on the first day you visited will begin to feel less disturbing.

And with your support, your mother, too, will probably adjust. She may enjoy watching all the activity that's going on around her. She may feel less isolated than she did before the move. She may make some friends. And she may appreciate knowing that she's not a burden to her family.

She could end up living in the nursing home for a long time, and for her it will become home. Both of you will know that it isn't the same as the home she knew before, but you may come to feel that it isn't so bad after all. By remaining actively involved in her life, you'll feel much better about the decision that you've made, and you'll know that you're doing the best you can in this less-than-perfect world.

Mary didn't respond to Kathleen's new approach right away. But Kathleen kept at it, and after several weeks, her mother's anger started to dissolve. Slowly she became her bossy old self again.

As her mother's attitude improved, Kathleen started to feel much more comfortable about the nursing home, and she was able to get on with her life. Now all she needed to do was manage to quit smoking again.

▼ Chapter
12

When Your Parent Is Dying

Joan was a clinical psychologist with a teenage daughter from a brief early marriage. She was distraught about her sixty-four-year-old mother, Lois.

Six years earlier her mother had been diagnosed with breast cancer and had undergone a radical mastectomy, radiation, and chemotherapy. The treatments were very hard on her, but she managed to endure them. Recently she'd had a checkup and learned that the cancer had recurred and spread. Her doctors offered her another course of chemotherapy, but they weren't optimistic about her chances. Lois was devastated by this terrible news, but for her there was really no question about what to do. She saw no point in putting herself through more suffering. All she wanted was to live out her life as fully as she could. She decided to quit her job and take a trip to Hawaii. She'd forego the chemotherapy.

Joan didn't begrudge her mother the well-deserved trip. Lois had been divorced when her children were young and had worked hard to support them without any help from their father. But Joan didn't want her mother to give up so easily. She did everything she could to convince her to change her mind about getting treatment. But Lois was firm in her decision.

When Your Parent Is Dying

The death of your parent is something that you know will happen some day, but when it does, it still can be devastating. It's hard for you to come to terms with the fact that your folks will be gone forever. They're irreplaceable, and you only have two of them. When they're gone, you're no longer someone's child, and there's no longer a generation that stands between you and death. You're next.

If your parent's death takes you by surprise, you're forced to deal with the reality of the situation immediately, and you have to get right down to the business of making funeral arrangements and straightening out her affairs.

But when you know that your parent is dying, the situation is different. You may live far away from her, and you may feel torn between wanting to be with her and wanting to be with your family at home. You may become tense every time you hear the phone ring because you're certain that this will be the call that tells you that she's either gotten worse or has died. You may never have been with someone who's dying, and you may be concerned about what's expected of you. And you may be apprehensive about what her death will be like.

Lois was glad that she took her trip when she did because a few months later, she was so weak she could barely get out of the house. She was eating little and had to be medicated for pain, and before long she had to hire someone to come in and help her with the household chores.

One evening, Joan got a call from her sister-in-law Bev. Bev was thinking of offering to come and care for Lois. She'd stayed with a friend who'd died of cancer a few years earlier, and because she was very fond of her mother-in-law, she wanted to do the same for her. She asked Joan if she wanted to join her.

Joan was caught off guard a little. She told Bev that she appreciated the fact that she was taking her feelings into consideration, but she explained that she was very angry with her mother for refusing treatment and that she didn't think she could bring herself to sit and watch her die. She admitted that her attitude may be wrong, but that was how she felt.

She told Bev that she should go ahead and stay with Lois if she wanted to.

The Hospice Movement

Until the past 50 years or so, people routinely died in their homes and were cared for by their families. However, because of recent advances in modern medical technology, many people who are gravely ill are now being brought to the hospital to receive treatment in the hope of extending their lives. But the fact is that much of the time, their quality of life is so poor that, given the choice, they would opt not to have treatment at all.

As a reaction to all of this, there has been a renewed awareness during the last few decades that death is part of the natural cycle of life and that prolonging life is not always in the dying person's best interest. The hospice movement is an outgrowth of that awareness.

The hospice concept was first developed in England in the 1960s. Its basic premise is that people should be able to die a dignified death in a loving environment. Hospice care emphasizes comfort measures rather than aggressive treatment. The patient as well as family members and friends are counseled and supported by a multidisciplinary team.

Many people in this country have been inspired by this idea, and hospice services have sprung up in many communities. These services are now integrated into the medical care system and are covered by Medicare, and sometimes by Medicaid and private health insurance.

Presently, hospice care is reserved primarily for cancer patients or for others who have life-threatening illnesses and who have very limited life expectancies. But this approach to patient care could be broadened to include other people as well. There are a great many frail, elderly people (many of them in nursing homes) who don't necessarily suffer from terminal illnesses but who have chronic health problems and are miserable nonetheless, and who don't wish to continue living. Perhaps they could be given the option of receiving comfort and support measures rather than aggressive treatment.

Joan's sister-in-law took care of Lois as Joan watched from the sidelines. Joan came up to see her mother every week or so, but her visits were brief, awkward, and superficial. She never spoke directly to Lois about the fact that she was dying, and she had a hard time even looking at her because she was still angry. Joan felt embarrassed that with all of her professional training, she didn't know how to handle herself better, and every time she left her mother's place, she felt that she'd let both her mother and herself down.

One afternoon as Joan started to leave, Bev asked her to sit down for awhile. Bev wanted to talk.

Joan stood there uneasily.

Bev told her that Joan's mother had mentioned how sad and disappointed she was that her daughter was so aloof and distant. Bev said that her mother wanted to talk with Joan about what was happening but that she didn't know how.

Joan didn't know what to say.

Bev went on, saying it was obvious that Joan was having a hard time accepting the fact that her mother was dying. Bev understood that, but added that in a few months Lois probably would be dead, and if Joan didn't spend the time well with her mother now, she might regret it for the rest of her life.

Joan tried to speak, but instead she started to cry.

Bev sat her sister-in-law down. They talked about the reasons for Joan's anger and how the anger was preventing her from being close to her mother during this critical time. As Joan listened to herself talk, she realized how frightened she was of losing her mother, but as they talked more, it became clear to her that she wanted to come and stay with Lois.

When you know that your parent is dying, you're faced with a significant loss, but you're also presented with an extraordinary opportunity.

The Bottom Line

If you make good use of the time you have left with your dying parent, you'll be giving your parent and yourself an extraordinary gift.

How to Make Good Use of the Time You Have Left with Your Dying Parent

Respond Directly and Honestly to Your Parent's Questions and Concerns

If you're not sure whether or not you should talk to your mother about the fact that she's dying, try to take your cues from her. She'll bring up the subject when she's ready. When you don't know how to respond to a particularly tough question, you can ask her what she thinks. You may be surprised by how much she knows. If she wants specific medical information, you can encourage her to ask her doctor directly, or you can help her find out what it is she wants to know. She'll ask for the truth when she's ready to hear it. And if she seems anxious and worried, try to help her identify exactly what it is that she's afraid of. There may be a simple answer that will calm her fears.

If she's not taking the initiative to talk openly about what's happening to her, you can try to get the conversation going by saying something like:

You look tired, Mom.

Or:

You're getting weaker, aren't you?

Openings like these will give her the message that it's okay for her to talk about what's going on. If she starts to share her feelings with you, all you have to do is listen to her. You can sit by her quietly and show with your facial expression and your body language that you're interested in hearing what she has to say. You can encourage her by nodding or by asking her a question. These are the kinds of conversations that can end up being meaningful and intimate.

Try to be Aware of Your Own Fears and Feelings of Discomfort so That They Don't Get in the Way

It's understandable that you may feel uncomfortable talking with your mother about the fact that she's dying. Because of your discomfort, you may be tempted to cut off the conversation when it becomes too awkward, to change the subject when it becomes too threatening, or to tell her not to talk about certain things because you don't want to hear about them. But if you let your own fears get in the way, she'll feel reluctant to talk to you about how she feels.

If you're ever tempted to lie to her, don't do it. If she finds out that you haven't been honest with her, the trust between you will be broken, and it will be difficult to re-establish. Besides, it's really not your right to deny her the opportunity to get her affairs in order and to prepare for her death. And it's usually a waste of energy to pretend that things are fine when they're not. If you and your other family members do this, your mother will feel isolated from all of you, and you'll feel the same way toward her. And everyone will have missed an opportunity for greater intimacy.

One way for you to get beyond your awkwardness is to tell her how you feel. You can say something like:

Mom, it's so hard for me to hear you talk about dying.

After you acknowledge this out loud, you may find that you feel more at ease talking with her.

If Your Parent Chooses to Deny the Truth, Try to be Understanding

It's important that you be honest with your mother, but there's no reason for you to take away her sense of hope. If she chooses not to accept the bad news, it's probably because she's not ready to hear it. If you try to force the truth on her, you can generate bad feelings; and, besides, she'll probably discount what you say anyway.

Her sense of hope may be serving a good purpose. It may give her the strength to carry on despite her illness, and it may be all that she has to cling to as she struggles to come to terms with this devastating loss.

Even when she says things that you know are totally unrealistic, there's no reason for you to shatter her illusions. You can show her that you understand her feelings without necessarily agreeing with her words. Instead of saying something like:

 Be realistic, Mom. June is six months from now. I can't imagine that you'll ever make the family reunion.

You can say something like:

 You'd really like to go to the family reunion in June, wouldn't you?

In the same way, if your mother wants to pursue a course of treatment that you consider to be useless, you should recognize that this is her right too. When people believe that a particular treatment will work, their confidence in it is thought to contribute to its success. And people sometimes do improve for reasons that nobody understands.

You can show her that you appreciate her desire to get better without actually supporting what you believe are false hopes by saying something like:

If you'd like to go to that clinic, I'll help you make the trip. But I just want you to know that I'm not convinced that they can do much more than the doctors here are doing.

This way you're not destroying her dreams, but you're also not holding out any unrealistic hopes for her either. If she wants to do something that she believes might help, she shouldn't be denied the opportunity to pursue it— even if it's a long shot. If she doesn't try, she may continue to question whether things could have turned out differently.

Consider Talking to Your Parent About the Option of Dying at Home

It may not be practical for you to care for your dying parent at home, and if it needs to be that she dies in a nursing home or in a hospital, you shouldn't feel that you've failed her. You can still take good advantage of the time you have left with her. But if it's feasible, you should give some thought to the possibility of having her die at home.

Many people don't realize that they can take care of their family members themselves and that very ill people don't have to die in the hospital. If you, your other parent, or other family members would like to care for your mother at home, you should speak with her and see how she feels about the idea.

173

Home has many advantages over an institutional setting. It's quieter and there's more privacy. The environment is more familiar and comfortable. Your mom will be surrounded by the people and the things that have given her life meaning. She can sleep in her own bed with whomever she's used to sleeping with. She can set her own schedule. She won't be subjected to medical procedures that have questionable value. She can have more control over how much medication she takes, and she can decide when she wants to take it. She can have as many visitors of any age as she wants, and they can come at any time of the day or night. And she can have her pets with her, too.

But you may be anxious about caring for your mother at home. You may never have taken care of a dependent adult before, and you may not know if you have what it takes to do it. You may be afraid that her death will be painful or grotesque, and you may be scared you won't react the way you should when it happens. You may worry that you won't hold up well if an emergency comes up. And you may not know if you'll be able to handle things if you need a nurse when one isn't immediately available.

These kinds of concerns are normal, and they shouldn't prevent you from going ahead with this option. If your mother chooses to die at home, a nurse and other staff members from a home health agency or a hospice organization will teach you and the other caregivers everything you'll need to know. They'll tell you what to expect as your mother gets closer to death. They'll teach you how to do bed care and how to perform any necessary procedures. They'll show you what to do if your mother experiences any discomfort. They'll explain what to do if there's a medical emergency. They'll answer any questions that you may have about how to involve young children in the experience. And they'll advise you about what to do when your mother's death occurs.

If you decide to go this route, you'll be taking on a big responsibility, and you may have to make substantial sacrifices. You'll probably have to take some time from your own life, and you may feel as though everything else is on hold. Furthermore, the physical demands of the job can be considerable, and there will be nights when you won't get much sleep. But despite the difficulties and the sadness, the experience of caring for a dying person can be deeply gratifying.

Most people who've had the courage to help a friend or a family member make the transition out of life feel very good about what they've done. The things that they were initially afraid of usually turn out to be far less intimidating and scary than what they'd imagined. And they almost always regard the experience as a rare privilege and as one of the high points of their lives.

Help Your Parent Take Care of Any Unfinished Business

Your mother may have some unfinished business that she'd like to take care of before she dies. You can help her with this by asking her if there's anyone whom she'd like to see, anything special that you can do for her, or anything else that she'd like to take care of that you might be able to help her with. She may want to see all of her children for one last time in order to say good-bye to them. She may want to patch things up with someone she hasn't spoken to in a long time. She may want to apologize to someone for something that she regrets having done. Or she may want to speak with a clergyperson about something that has been troubling her.

You can also make it your business to attend to any unfinished business of your own that you still have with your mother. The knowledge that she'll die soon may finally give you the incentive to say something to her that you may have wanted to say before but haven't. This is your last opportunity to make peace with her and to tell her that you love her. If you make the effort to resolve any lingering problems that exist between you, you'll both feel much better, and the two of you may be able to establish a new closeness. Try to do this while your mom can still understand you and respond to you. If you don't speak up now, you may always wish you had.

Give Your Parent Opportunities to Reminisce About the Past

Many dying people like to look back over their lives as death gets closer, but sometimes their family members discourage this kind of talk because they think that it's an indication that their minds are failing. Actually it's an important step in the process of coming to terms with death and in letting go.

When you show an interest in your mother's past, you're giving her a big psychological boost. You're honoring her and telling her that you appreciate and recognize her unique qualities. As you reminisce together, you can help her see that her life has been worthwhile and that she has made a contribution. This can help her achieve a greater sense of inner peace and self-acceptance.

Reminiscing can be good for you, too. As you learn more about her life, there's a greater likelihood that you'll be able to accept her as she is, and you'll learn to appreciate the values and forces that made you what you are. And you'll probably find that this acceptance will help your relationship become closer.

Be Physical with Your Parent

Almost everyone enjoys physical contact. Touching helps people feel more alive and connected to each other. If the members of your family haven't been particularly demonstrative in the past, you still have the opportunity to change things. Being physical with your mother can help break down the old barriers that may exist between you.

Start slowly and do what feels right to you. You may be pleasantly surprised by your mom's response.

176

Allow Yourself to Cry

Crying is a natural way for the body to release strong emotions, and a good cry can leave you with a rich feeling of deep, quiet calm. If you continually suppress your tears, your feelings will find other more destructive ways of expressing themselves, such as tense muscles or angry behavior.

If you get the urge to cry, you shouldn't hesitate to do so in front of your parent. You may be afraid that it will upset her. You may hold back because you're worried that you'll come across as weak or out of control. You may hesitate because you're afraid that you'll look unattractive. And you may think that if you start to cry, you won't be able to stop. But when you cry in your mom's presence, you're giving her permission to cry too. And when you cry together, you can break down the sense of isolation that both of you may be feeling. Tears can convey a depth of emotion that words sometimes can't.

If you don't feel comfortable crying in front of your mother, try to find someone else to cry with, or let yourself cry alone.

Keep Communicating with Your Parent up to the Very End

When your mother is close to death, you can continue to talk to her even though you're not completely sure that she can hear or understand you. It may give her a great deal of comfort to hear your voice.

Don't say things in front of her that you don't want her to hear because you can never know for sure what's getting through to her. Even when she sounds confused, communication still can take place. If you listen carefully, you may discover a certain imagery behind her words. She may say things like, "I want to get out of here," or "Let's go for a ride."

Taken literally, these things may not make a lot of sense. But what she may be trying to say is that she's ready to die. If you respond to the feelings behind her words, you may find that you can strike a responsive chord in her. You can reply to her by saying something like:

 You're tired of being here, Mom. You're ready to go, aren't you?

Try to Let go of Your Idealized Expectations of the Perfect Death Experience

Your mother's death may not turn out exactly the way you wanted it to. You may take time off from your job and leave your family on their own so that you can be with her during her last weeks. But she may not die when she's expected to, and you may have to go back home before she does.

During the time you spend with your mom, you may never achieve a satisfying sense of closure with her. Your own fears or anxieties may be too overwhelming. The mood may never be quite right. She may make it too difficult for you to open up. Or you may want to be with her during her last moments, and so you may sit by her bed and wait. But then, when you leave for a short period of time, she may die.

Try not to berate yourself if things don't work out as you'd hoped they would. Remind yourself that you did the best you could, and be proud of what you've accomplished. Take pride in the time that you spent with your mother and in the care that you gave her. She may not have had the wherewithal to thank you, but that shouldn't take away from the fact that your care and your presence have enriched her life.

At first, Joan felt apprehensive about staying with her mother, but she quickly got over it, and the next four weeks flew by. She and Lois had some good talks, they reminisced together, and they laughed too. The experience wasn't nearly as morbid or depressing as Joan had feared it would be.

The hospice nurse came by to monitor Lois's vital signs, to make sure that her pain medication was adequate, and to help prepare the family for what lay ahead; the rest of the hospice team also visited. Everyone in the family felt cared for and supported.

Lois deteriorated rapidly. Toward the end she was literally skin and bones, and her pain got so bad that she had to be medicated constantly.

When it appeared that she didn't have much time left, Joan's brother, his kids, and Joan's daughter came to stay. Lois drifted in and out of consciousness; as her death approached, she couldn't be aroused, her extremities became cold, and her breathing became irregular.

During her last hours, her body shook noisily with every breath. Joan was dozing in an easy chair by Lois' bed when she woke up with a start and realized that the room was quiet and that her mother's body finally was still.

Allow Yourself to Mourn the Death of Your Parent

Nothing can completely prepare you for the death of your parent. No matter how expected it is, it will come as a shock—even if she has suffered terribly and even if you've fervently wished for the ordeal to be over.

Although her death will release you from the responsibility and burden of caregiving, you still have your grief to face. Grief is an unpleasant, empty feeling, and you may have trouble dealing with it. You may try to distract yourself by running from one activity to another, by overeating, or by numbing yourself with alcohol or drugs.

These tactics may work for the moment, but avoiding the pain won't give you a chance to experience your grief. With each additional (and inevitable) loss that you go through, your suppressed feelings will overwhelm you even more, and you'll become increasingly afraid to let them out. This is one reason why funerals and memorial services are so important. They give people permission to mourn. The sooner you allow yourself to grieve, the sooner you'll be free to go on with your life.

If your parent has died and you still have some unfinished business to take care of, it may help you if you write her a letter that says all of the things that you'd have liked to have said to her. And if you think that you need some extra help during this period, you might want to consider getting counseling or joining a bereavement support group.

At her mother's funeral, Joan felt a great deal of sadness that her mother had died when she was still relatively young. And she had to admit that there was some anger left inside of her. But basically, she felt good because she'd come through for her mother . . . and for herself.

Epilogue

The Up Side

When you were younger, you probably gave very little thought to what might happen when your parents got old. So parentcare may be something that you didn't exactly count on (not that you could have prepared for it even if you tried). By now you've probably learned that helping your folks through their later years is a bittersweet experience.

Sometimes parents become so ill or their spirits become so beaten down that life no longer holds any joy for them at all. And sometimes children knock themselves out for their folks and get very little in return. In these kinds of situations, the difficulties seem to overshadow everything else.

Even under happier circumstances, adult children can't help but feel some pain and sadness as they watch their parents grow frail and become increasingly dependent on them.

But there's an up side to all of this, as well.

You're fortunate that your folks have lived long enough to see you grow into an independent, productive person. And if you have children, they may be blessed with grandparents who've enriched their lives. You're also lucky if you

181

and your brothers and sisters have had the chance to gain new respect and appreciation for each other as you've worked together to help your parents.

But perhaps best of all, you've had the opportunity to establish an adult relationship—and maybe a real friendship—with your parents. You've been in a position to treat them with the love, generosity, and tenderness that can heal old wounds. By relying on you, they've shown you that they recognize certain capabilities in you and that they trust you.

Not everyone has this good fortune.

It's especially important that you look after yourself so that the difficulties and the frustrations don't overwhelm you. That way, both you and your parents will be better able to make the most of the time that you have left together.

Part III

The Extras

Nifty Gifts

It's easy to think of gift ideas for some people, but for others, it can be a real chore. Your parents may not particularly like to receive gifts. They may claim that they have everything they need. They may insist that they don't want any money spent on them. They may not want you to go to any trouble for them. They may seem to have everything they need, and you may have a hard time coming up with something that's unique and that they actually could use.

But in spite of all this, there will be times when you'll want to give your folks a nice gift, something thoughtful that lets them know that you're thinking about them and that you care.

The trick is to come up with a fresh idea. Here are a few good gifts to consider:

- a gift of your time—an afternoon at a concert, a play, or a sporting event; a drive and a picnic in the country; a vacation together

- framed photos or framed artwork done by the grandchildren

- a family photo collage

- a purse-size photo album with family photos in it

- large print books or magazines

- a magazine subscription

- a book for writing down memories (such as *Grandmother Remembers: A Written Heirloom for My Grandchild* by Judith Levy)

- an extension phone (allows couples to speak on the phone at the same time and makes answering the phone more convenient)

- a new phone with touch tone, adjustable volume control, and/or phone number memory

- a cordless phone

- a videocassette recorder (VCR)
- audiocassettes or videocassettes of the grandchildren
- a tape recorder
- books on tape or a books on tape mail-order catalog
- cassettes of favorite old radio shows
- a compact disc player
- cassettes or compact discs of favorite music
- a television set with remote control
- an indoor/outdoor thermometer
- a weather station
- a bird feeder, birdseed, a bird identification book, and binoculars
- a parakeet or a canary along with a cage and some food
- a starter set for a stamp or coin collection
- a wood carving, wood burning, or woodworking kit
- rug hooking, needlecraft, or other arts and crafts supplies
- games to play alone or to play with others (some are available in large print format)
- a magnifying glass or a page magnifier
- a crossword puzzle book along with a crossword puzzle dictionary
- a paint-by-number set
- cut flowers
- a seasonal wreath
- plants, gardening supplies, a seed catalog
- personalized note paper and return address labels

- assorted greeting cards
- a calendar with dates of special occasions marked on it
- any home-made or home-grown food item
- membership in a fruit-of-the-month club
- a mobile for a bedridden patient
- a storage unit for under the bed
- a bed tray
- an orthopedic pillow
- a clock with large numbers and an illuminated face, or a talking clock
- a decorative night light
- satin-covered clothes hangers
- a deluxe shoeshine kit
- a gift certificate for a manicure, a pedicure, a facial, or a massage
- a T-shirt or sweatshirt with a picture of grandchildren printed on the front
- a pair of slippers, a bed jacket, a nightgown, pajamas, or a bathrobe
- a warm-up suit
- a fanny pack
- a saddlebag for use with a wheelchair or a walker
- a pill cutter or grinder
- a divided pillbox
- a subscription to a personal emergency response system
- sheepskin seat covers for the car
- a YMCA or health club membership

Useful Names and Numbers

There are a number of organizations around the country that will give you useful information about many of the problems that your parents may have. Many of them will send you free or low-cost brochures, and many of them also offer annual memberships that include bimonthly or quarterly newsletters that keep members up on the latest developments in their respective areas of interest.

General Information on the Issues of Aging

American Association of Retired Persons
601 E Street NW
Washington, DC 20049
(202) 434-2277

Although this group concerns itself primarily with retirement issues, it publishes a variety of practical booklets related to parentcare that are available free of charge. Call or write to them to get a list.

National Association of Area Agencies on Aging
1112 16th Street NW
Suite 100
Washington, DC 20036
(202) 296-8130

This office represents more than 650 area agencies that have been mandated by Congress to help older people take advantage of the social and medical services that are available to them. Because the names of the local agencies vary from community to community, it's sometimes difficult to find their phone numbers. You can call or send a postcard to the national office to get the phone number of the agency nearest you.

National Rehabilitation and Information Center/
ABLEDATA
8455 Colesville Road
Suite 935
Silver Spring, MD 20910
(800) 346-2742 voice/TDD
(301) 588-9284
(301) 587-1967 Fax

These two organizations currently operate out of the same office. NARIC maintains a computer database that contains information on the latest research on all aspects of disability and rehabilitation. ABLEDATA helps people locate distributors for more than 15,000 commercially available assistive devices.

Resources for Adult Children of Aging Parents

Aging Network Services
4400 East-West Highway
Suite 907
Bethesda, MD 20814
(301) 657-4329

This private, nationwide service will do an extensive family assessment by phone and will then match people up with qualified clinical social workers in their areas. This could be particularly valuable for long-distance caregivers.

Children of Aging Parents
Woodbourne Office Campus
Suite 302A
1609 Woodbourne Road
Levittown, PA 19057
(215) 945-6900

The national office will connect you with a support group in your area. They can provide you with valuable information and emotional support.

National Association of Private Geriatric Care Managers
655 N. Alvernon Way
Suite 108
Tucson, AZ 85711
(602) 881-8008
(602) 325-7925 Fax

They maintain a list of private geriatric care managers who meet their quality standards, and they'll send you names of members who practice in your parents' area.

Medical Problems

Alzheimer's Association
919 N. Michigan Avenue
Suite 1000
Chicago, IL 60611
(800) 272-3900 (outside IL)
(800) 572-6037 (in IL)
(312) 853-3060

They'll send a generous packet of written information containing the basic facts on Alzheimer's disease, and they'll direct you to your local chapters where you can get guidance and emotional support.

American Cancer Society
1599 Clifton Road NE
Atlanta, GA 30329
(800) ACS-2345

The local offices offer a variety of services including support groups for families, volunteer visitors for breast cancer patients, a lending library of books and videos, transportation programs, and assistance in obtaining medical equipment. Check the white pages of your phone directory for the number of your local office, or call the national office to get the location of the chapter nearest you.

American Diabetes Association
1660 Duke Street
Alexandria, VA 22314
(800) 232-3472

They offer information that covers all aspects of diabetes management, and they refer people to physicians and other resources in their areas. Check the white pages of your phone book or call the national office to find your nearest chapter.

American Heart Association
7272 Greenville Avenue
Dallas, TX 75231
(214) 373-6300

Local chapters provide educational materials on the prevention of heart disease and its warning signs. Look in the white pages of your telephone directory or contact the national office to find your nearest chapter.

American Lung Association
1740 Broadway
New York, NY 10019
(212) 315-8700

Chapters in all major cities offer smoking cessation programs. They also sponsor educational programs about lung problems for patients and their family members. And in addition, they put out a variety of free publications.

American Podiatric Medical Association
9312 Old Georgetown Road
Bethesda, MD 20814
(800) FOOTCARE
(301) 571-9200

Podiatrists are doctors who specialize in the diagnosis and treatment of foot injuries and disease. You can call the national office to obtain free brochures on foot problems. They'll also give you the phone number of your state branch where you can get referrals to local podiatrists.

American Society for Geriatric Dentistry
211 E. Chicago Avenue
16th Floor
Chicago, IL 60611
(312) 440-2660

The members of this group specialize in dental care for the elderly. They'll refer you to their members who practice in your parents' area.

Arthritis Foundation
P.O. Box 1900
Atlanta, GA 30326
(800) 283-7800

The national office sends out free informative brochures and will tell you where you can find local chapters. The local chapters sponsor exercise programs, support groups, and classes in arthritis management. They also make physician referrals.

Help for Incontinent People
P.O. Box 544
Union, SC 29329
(803) 579-7900
(803) 579-7902 Fax

They send out educational material on problems related to incontinence.

National Stroke Association
300 E. Hampden Avenue
Suite 240
Englewood, CO 80110
(800) 787-6537
(303) 762-9922
(303) 762-1190 FAX

The group publishes two books for stroke survivors and their families. They're titled *The Road Ahead: A Stroke Recovery Guide* and *Family Caregiver's Guide.* They also put out a listing of companies that manufacture adaptive equipment, special clothing, and other products that are useful for stroke survivors.

Simon Foundation
P.O. Box 815
Wilmette, IL 60091
(800) 237-4666
(708) 864-3913

This group publishes a book for laypeople that's titled *Managing Incontinence: A Guide to Living With the Loss of Bladder Control.* It may be in your local library, or you can purchase it directly from them.

All five of the following Parkinson's organizations publish newsletters, send out brochures, and make referrals to local support groups and physicians. Some of these groups are in the process of merging, as of this writing.

American Parkinson Disease Association
60 Bay Street
Staten Island, NY 10301
(800) 223-2732
(718) 981-8001

California Parkinson's Foundation
2444 Moorpark Avenue
Suite 316
San Jose, CA 95128
(800) 786-2958 (outside CA)
(800) 655-2273 (in CA)
(408) 998-8366

National Parkinson Foundation, Inc.
1501 NW 9th Avenue
Bob Hope Road
Miami, FL 33136
(800) 327-4545 (outside FL)
(800) 433-7022 (in FL)
(800) 400-8448 (in CA)
(305) 547-6666
(305) 548-4403 Fax

Parkinson's Disease Foundation
650 W. 168th Street
New York, NY 10032
(800) 457-6676
(212) 923-4700

United Parkinson Foundation
360 W. Superior Street
Chicago, IL 60610
(312) 664-2344

Sensory Impairment

American Foundation for the Blind, Inc.
Product Center
100 Enterprise Place
P.O. Box 7044
Dover, DE 19903
(800) 829-0500
(800) 676-3299 Fax
(302) 677-6700

They'll mail out a catalog titled *Products for People with Vision Problems.* It features many items for recreational use along with numerous useful aids to independent living.

National Association for the Visually Handicapped
22 W. 21st Street
New York, NY 10010
(212) 889-3141
(212) 727-2931 Fax

This group serves the partially seeing population. It runs a free-by-mail large-print lending library of more than 1600 titles, publishes a large-print weekly news magazine, and puts out a visual aids catalog in large-print format.

National Eye Care Project
P.O. Box 429098
San Francisco, CA 94142
(800) 222-EYES

This project is sponsored by the American Academy of Ophthalmology. They'll send you names of ophthalmologists around the country who'll provide free or low-cost care to financially disadvantaged older adults. They also put out easy-to-read brochures about eye conditions that commonly affect people over age sixty-five.

Modern Talking Picture Service
5000 Park Street North
St. Petersburg, FL 33709
(800) 237-6213

This organization is under contract with the U.S. Department of Education. They'll mail you a catalog that lists 3,000 captioned films of all types for hearing-impaired people. The films can be borrowed postage-free.

National Information Center on Deafness
Gallaudet University
Kendall Green
800 Florida Avenue NE
Washington, DC 20002
(202) 651-5051
(202) 651-5052 TDD
(202) 651-5054 Fax

This center acts as a clearinghouse for all of the national, not-for-profit organizations that provide information, special devices, and educational services for deaf and hard-of-hearing people.

National Library Service for the Blind and Physically Handicapped
The Library of Congress
1291 Taylor Street NW
Washington, DC 20542
(800) 424-8567
(202) 707-5100
(202) 707-0712 Fax

This service, known as Talking Books, provides a postage-free mail-order library service that offers books, periodicals, and music on audiocassette to people who can't see well enough to read conventional print or who have another physical disability that prevents them from using printed material.

Mental Health

Al-Anon Family Group Headquarters, Inc.
P.O. Box 862 Midtown Station
New York, NY 10018
(800) 356-9996

Al-Anon has been in existence since 1951 and has more than 32,000 groups in 104 countries. They run support groups for relatives and friends of alcoholics and will direct you to a support group near you. They'll also send you a list of reading material that you can order.

American Association for Geriatric Psychiatry
P.O. Box 376A
Greenbelt, MD 20770
(301) 220-0952

This is a nationwide organization of over 1300 psychiatrists who specialize in treating mental disorders of the elderly. They can refer you to their members who practice in your parent's area.

American Psychiatric Association
1400 K Street NW
Washington, DC 20005
(202) 682-6000

They'll send you free copies of their pamphlets that discuss various psychiatric disorders, as well as mental health problems, that are often seen in the elderly.

Legal and Financial Issues

Health Insurance Association of America
National Insurance Consumer Helpline
1025 Connecticut Avenue NW
Washington, DC 20036
(800) 942-4242

Trained personnel and licensed agents are available to assist consumers who have questions about insurance matters. They also send out informative written material and refer consumer complaints to the appropriate agencies.

Institute of Certified Financial Planners
7600 E. Eastman Avenue
Suite 301
Denver, CO 80231
(800) 282-PLAN

They'll send you the names along with the qualifications of three financial planners in your area. They'll also send a brochure titled "Selecting a Qualified Financial Planning Professional: Twelve Questions to Consider."

National Academy of Elder Law Attorneys, Inc.
655 N. Alvernon Way
Suite 108
Tucson, AZ 85711
(602) 881-4005

The group will make local referrals and send a free, helpful pamphlet.

National Center for Home Equity Conversion
1210 East College Drive
Suite 300
Marshall, MN 56258
(507) 532-3230

If you send them a self-addressed, stamped envelope along with $1, they'll send you back a "Reverse Mortgage Locator" that will tell you about the different home equity conversion plans that are available in your parents' state. They also sell a book titled *Retirement Income on the House.*

Housing

National Shared Housing Resource Center
136½ Main Street
Montpelier, VT 05602
(802) 223-2627

The center maintains a list of approximately 400 shared housing programs in 42 states. They'll tell you about programs in your parents' area, and they'll send you a helpful free booklet called "A Consumer's Guide to Homesharing."

National Citizens' Coalition for Nursing Home Reform
1224 M Street NW
Suite 301
Washington, DC 20005
(202) 393-2018
(202) 393-4122 Fax

They'll give you the address and phone number of the Long-Term Care Ombudsman's office in your parents' state. This is the office to contact if you have an unresolved complaint regarding any licensed long-term care facility.

Death and Dying

Choice in Dying, Inc.
200 Varick Street
10th Floor
New York, NY 10014
(212) 366-5540

Two groups, Concern for Dying and Society for the Right to Die, have merged to form this new organization. They offer information about the issues that people face as death approaches and about the rights of patients and their families to control treatment decisions. They'll send you a copy of the advanced medical directive that's used in your state.

Make Today Count, Inc.
P.O. Box 6063
Kansas City, KS 66106
(913) 362-2866

Local chapters give information and emotional support to people with life-threatening illnesses and to their caregivers and family members.

National Hospice Organization
1901 N. Moore Street
Suite 901
Arlington, VA 22209
(800) 658-8898
(703) 243-5900
(703) 525-5762 Fax

They provide information about hospice insurance benefits and will make referrals to hospice services in your parents' area.

Recommended Reading

(by subject)

Making Peace With Your Parents: The Key to Enriching Your Life and All Your Relationships
by Harold H. Bloomfield, M.D. with Leonard Felder, Ph.D.
Ballantine Books, 1983

Talks about the difficulties that adult children commonly have with their parents and presents practical ways to improve the relationship.

Guilt is the Teacher, Love is the Lesson
by Joan Borysenko, Ph.D.
Warner Books, 1990

If the Old Guilt Routine is a problem for you, then you should read this book. It talks about the roots of guilt, and discusses how to forgive yourself and others so that you can get on with your life.

Dance of Anger: A Woman's Guide to Changing the Patterns of Intimate Relationships
by Harriet Goldhow Lerner, Ph.D.
Harper & Row, 1985

The anger that some people feel toward their parents continues throughout adulthood. This book explains how to turn anger into a constructive force that can reshape your life.

The Caregiver's Guide: Helping Elderly Relatives Cope with Health & Safety Problems
by Caroline Robb, R.N., with Janet Reynolds, G.N.P.
Houghton Mifflin Company, 1991

This useful reference book talks in understandable language about the health problems common to elderly people. It recommends some simple things you can do and explains how to know if a problem is serious enough that it requires medical attention.

Keys to Planning for Long-Term Custodial Care
by David Ness
Barron's Educational Series, Inc., 1991

A useful book for parents who are interested in making plans for the time when they may need help. Discusses strategies that can save them money, maximize the return on their assets, and give them a sense of security and peace of mind.

Everything Your Heirs Need to Know: Your Assets, Family History and Final Wishes
by David S. Magee
Dearborn Financial Publishing, Inc., 1991

A clever book that might make a good gift for your parents. It includes forms on which they can enter information about themselves and their assets, spaces for writing their burial and funeral wishes, and cardboard pockets for filing copies of their important documents. If your parents did everything that the book recommends, things would be much easier on you.

Guide to Independent Living for People with Arthritis
The Arthritis Foundation, 1988

This comprehensive manual describes hundreds of useful assistive devices. It's exceptionally well-organized and offers information that will help any disabled person manage better in every room of the house. It can be purchased from your local Arthritis Foundation for only $5.

Eighty-Eight Easy-To-Make Aids for Older People
by Don Caston
Hartley & Marks, Inc., 1988

If you can use a few basic tools, you can make these simple aids for your folks. The book is clearly illustrated and gives step-by-step instructions.

To Be Old and Sad: Understanding Depression in the Elderly
by Nathan Billig, M.D.
Lexington Books, 1987

A lucid, nontechnical book that shows how to recognize serious depression in the elderly and explains what can be done about it.

Caring for the Mentally Impaired Elderly: A Family Guide
by Florence Safford
Henry Holt and Company, 1986

A clearly-written, practical, compassionate book that tells you just about everything you need to know about dementia.

Understanding Difficult Behaviors: Some Practical Suggestions for Coping with Alzheimer's Disease and Related Illnesses
Alzheimer's Association of South Central Michigan
P.O. Box 1713
Ann Arbor, MI 48106

This useful manual explains how to deal with the difficult behavior of demented people. Invaluable for families struggling to take care of a demented person at home. You can order a copy from the above address, or you can get one from your local Alzheimer's Association.

The Nursing Home Experience: A Family Guide to Making It Better
by Marylou Hughes
Crossroad, 1992

There are several good books that discuss how to choose a nursing home, but this one talks in depth about the feelings and concerns of the family members of residents. It suggests ways to make visits as pleasant as possible and shows how to help your parents feel more at home in an institutional setting.

Easing the Passage: A Guide for Prearranging and Ensuring a Pain-Free and Tranquil Death via a Living Will, Personal Medical Mandate, and Other Medical, Legal, and Ethical Resources
by David E. Outerbridge and Alan R. Hersh, M.D.
Harper Perennial, 1991

An excellent book for anyone who wonders whether or not to complete an advanced medical directive. This is a good gift for a skeptical parent.

Keeping Family Stories Alive: A Creative Guide to Taping Your Family Life and Lore
by Vera Rosenbluth
Hartley & Marks, Inc., 1990

This is the book to use if you want to do an audio or video tape of your parents as they talk about their lives. It gives tips on interviewing and provides a list of questions that will help get you started.

Coming Home: A Guide to Dying at Home with Dignity
by Deborah Duda
Aurora Press, 1987

A personal book that was written from the heart. It talks about making a dying person's final weeks as comfortable and meaningful as possible.

When Parents Die: A Guide for Adults
by Edward Myers
Penguin Books, 1987

This sensitive guide can help adult children get through the often difficult experience of a parent's death.

Books for Young Children

Now One Foot, Now the Other
by Tomie de Paola
G. P. Putnam's Sons, 1981

When Bobby is a baby, his grandfather teaches him how to walk. Then when Bobby is five, his grandfather has a stroke. Now it's Bobby's turn to help his grandfather.

Grandpa Doesn't Know It's Me
by Donna Guthrie
Human Sciences Press, Inc., 1986

Lizzie's grandfather has Alzheimer's disease and moves in with her family when he can no longer live alone.

My Grandma's in a Nursing Home
by Judy Delton and Dorothy Tucker
Albert Whitman & Company, 1986

At first Jason finds it difficult to visit his elderly grandmother in a nursing home, but eventually he learns to enjoy his visits.

Nana Upstairs & Nana Downstairs
by Tomie de Paola
Puffin Books, 1988

Tommy's great-grandmother dies, and he comes to see that death is part of the natural cycle of life.

Additional Books

The following titles, available from Barron's Educational Series, Inc., will be of interest to older people and to their caregivers.

Barron's Keys to Retirement Planning

Keys to Buying a Retirement Home
Keys to Choosing a Doctor
Keys to Dealing with the Loss of a Loved One
Keys to Fitness Over Fifty
Keys to Living with a Retired Husband
Keys to Medications and Drug Interactions
Keys to Menopause and Beyond
Keys to Nutrition Over Fifty
Keys to Planning for Long-Term Custodial Care
Keys to Preparing a Will
Keys to Survival for Caregivers
Keys to Understanding Alzheimer's Disease
Keys to Understanding Arthritis
Keys to Understanding Medicare
Keys to Understanding Osteoporosis
Keys to Understanding Social Security Benefits

Barron's Business Keys

Keys to Avoiding Probate and Reducing Estate Taxes
Keys to Estate Planning and Trusts
Keys to Retirement Planning

A Handbook for Creative Retirement Planning

Life Begins at 50

Index

About the Authors

Enid Pritikin is the supervisor of social services at the Santa Barbara Visiting Nurse Association and has worked with elderly people and their families for more than 20 years. In addition, she consults in nursing homes, teaches adult education classes, and conducts seminars on parentcare issues. She lives in a family compound with her parents, husband, and two sons.

Trudy Reece is an occupational therapist and freelance journalist who has written for a number of newspapers and magazines. She lives with her husband and two children in Santa Barbara. Enid and Trudy have been friends since they were twelve.